the BEST JOKE BOOK Ever

Wayne Brindle

CONTENTS

All God's Creatures

One day, while driving in the countryside, a salesman saw a chicken running alongside his car. He appeared to have three legs. And he was fast. The traveler sped up to fifty miles per hour, and the chicken stayed right with him. At eighty he was still there, jogging his little heart out, staring at the driver with a smirk on his beak. The motorist decided to stop and take a closer look when all of a sudden the chicken darted into a farm driveway and disappeared. He slammed on his brakes and backed up. As he drove up to the farmhouse, an old man walked out with his wife and teenage son.

"Hey, have y'all seen a three-legged chicken around here?"

"Sure," the farmer said. "That's my chicken."

"Really? How'd he get three legs? He's really fast on his feet!"

The old man spat into the dirt. "My wife and son and I live here alone. We don't have much to eat but we all love fried chicken, especially the drumsticks. I finally decided to develop a new breed of chicken with three legs, so we could each have a drumstick from only one chicken."

"Amazing! How do they taste?"

"I don't know," he said. "We haven't been able to catch him yet."

* * *

A cat ate some cheese and waited in front of a mousehole with bated breath.

* * *

A family of skunks went for their morning walk. They came to a fork in the road.

The daddy skunk said, "My instinct tells me to take the left fork."

The momma skunk said, "My instinct tells me to take the right fork."

The baby skunk pondered a moment and said, "My end stinks too but I still don't know which road to take!"

* * *

Our teacher asked us what our favorite animal was, and I said, "Fried chicken." She said I wasn't funny, but she couldn't have been right, because everyone else in the class laughed. I told my dad what happened, and he said my teacher was probably a member of PETA. He said they love animals very much.

I do, too. Especially chicken, pork and beef. Anyway, my teacher sent me to the principal's office. I told him what happened, and he laughed, too. Then he told me not to do it again. The next day in class my teacher asked me what my favorite live animal was. I told her it was chicken. She asked me why, just like she'd asked the other children. So I told her it was because you could make them into fried chicken.

She sent me back to the principal's office again. He laughed, and told me not to do it again. I don't understand. My parents taught me to be honest, but my teacher doesn't like it when I am. Today, my teacher asked us to tell her what famous person we admire most.

I told her, "Colonel Sanders." Guess where I am now.

* * *

A woman hiking in Yellowstone Park was chased by a grizzly bear, and she ran to a ranger station where she was arrested by park rangers. It's illegal to run through the park with a bear behind.

* * *

A crow was sitting on a tree, doing nothing all day. A small rabbit saw the crow, and asked him, "Can I also sit like you and do nothing all day long?"

The crow answered, "Sure, why not?"

So, the rabbit sat on the ground below the crow, and rested. All of a sudden, a fox appeared, jumped on the rabbit and ate it.

The moral of the story is: To be sitting and doing nothing, you must be sitting very, very high up.

* * *

A Baptist preacher and his wife decided to get a new dog. Ever mindful of the congregation, they knew the dog must also be a Baptist. They visited kennel after kennel and explained their needs. Finally, they found a kennel whose owner assured them he had just the dog they wanted. The owner brought the dog to meet the pastor and his wife. "Fetch the Bible," he commanded. The dog bounded to the bookshelf, scrutinized the books, located the Bible, and brought it to the owner. "Now find Psalm 23," he commanded. The dog dropped the Bible to the floor, and showing marvelous dexterity with his paws, leafed through, found the correct passage, and pointed to it with his paw. The pastor and his wife were very impressed and purchased the dog.

That evening, a group of church members came to visit. The pastor and his wife began to show off the dog, having him locate several Bible verses. The visitors were very impressed. One man asked, "Can he do regular dog tricks, too?"

"I haven't tried yet," the pastor replied. He pointed his finger at the dog. "Heel!" the pastor commanded. The dog immediately jumped on a chair, placed one paw on the pastor's forehead and began to howl. The pastor looked at his wife in shock and said, "Oh my! He's Pentecostal!"

* * *

A fellow had a pet buzzard named Buford and decided to take him to Hawaii on vacation. He realized it was a long flight and that he couldn't afford the exorbitant fees charged by airlines for extra luggage. So he bought Buford a ticket. But the airline denied boarding to Buford. It seems Buford had too much carrion baggage.

* * *

A research group on sea mammals captured a rather odd porpoise on one of its trips. Its peculiarity was that it had feet. After they had photographed and measured the poor thing, they prepared to set it free.

"Wait a minute," said one of the researchers, "wouldn't it be a kindness if our ship's doctor here were to amputate the feet so that it would be like other porpoises?"

"Not on your life," exclaimed the doctor. "That would be defeeting the porpoise."

* * *

A couple goes for a meal at a Chinese restaurant and orders the "Chicken Surprise." The waiter brings the meal, served in a lidded cast-iron pot. Just as the wife is about to serve herself, the lid of the pot rises slightly and she briefly sees two beady little eyes looking around before the lid slams back down.

"Good grief, did you see that?" she asks her husband.

He hasn't, so she asks him to look in the pot. He reaches for it and again the lid rises, and he sees two little eyes looking around before it slams down.

Sputtering in a fit of pique, he calls the waiter over, describes what is happening, and demands an explanation!

"Please sir," says the waiter, "what did you order?"

The husband replies, "Chicken Surprise."

"Ah . . . so sorry," says the waiter, "I brought you Peeking Duck."

* * *

A three-legged dog walks into a bar and says to the bartender, "I'm looking for the dirty varmint that shot my paw."

* * *

A little girl was talking to her teacher about whales. The teacher said it was physically impossible for a whale to swallow a human because even though it was a very large mammal, its throat was very small. The little girl stated that Jonah was swallowed by a whale. Irritated, the teacher reiterated that a whale could not swallow a human; it was physically impossible.

The little girl said, "When I get to heaven I will ask Jonah."

The teacher asked, "What if Jonah went to hell?"

The little girl replied, "Then you ask him."

* * *

Some race horses are in a stable. One of them starts to boast about his track record. "In the last 15 races, I've won 8 of them!"

Another horse breaks in, "Well in the last 27 races, I've won 19!"

"Oh, that's good, but in the last 36 races, I've won 28!" says another, flicking his tail.

At this point, they notice that a greyhound dog has been sitting there listening. "I don't mean to boast," says the greyhound, "but in my last 90 races, I've won 88 of them!"

The horses are clearly amazed. "Wow!" says one, after a hushed silence. "A talking dog!"

* * *

A duck went into a pharmacy and told the pharmacist he needed some Chapstick.

The pharmacist asked, "Are you paying cash?"

The duck said, "No, just put it on my bill."

* * *

"I shot my dog."

"Was he mad?"

"Well, it didn't seem to exactly please him."

* * *

A blind man with his seeing eye dog walked into a bar. He picked up the dog by the tail and swung it around and around over his head.

The bartender ran up and asked, "Dude, what are you doing?"

The blind man replied, "Just looking around."

* * *

A guy walks into a bar and sees a dog playing poker. The guy is amazed that the dog is playing poker.

"Bartender, is that a real dog playing poker?" the guy asks.

"Yep, real as can be." the bartender replies.

"Well, is he any good?" the guy asks.

"Na, every time he has a good hand he wags his tail."

* * *

A man was driving down a backcountry road in the middle of ranch country when his car stalled. He got out and raised the hood to see if he could find out what had happened. A brown, white-faced cow slowly lumbered from the field she had been grazing in over to the car and stuck her head under the hood beside the man. After a moment the cow looked at the man and said, "Looks like a bad carburetor to me." Then she walked back into the field and began grazing again.

Amazed, the man walked back to the ranch house he had just passed, where he met a rancher. "Hey, mister, is that your cow in the field?" he asked.

The rancher looked out where he pointed and replied, "Yep, that's old Bessie."

The man said, "Well, my car's broken down, and she walks over, looks under the hood and says, 'Looks like a bad carburetor to me.'"

The rancher shook his head and said, "Don't mind old Bessie, son. She hangs around the garage, reads a couple of magazines, and thinks she knows everything—actually she don't know a thing about carburetors."

* * *

A frog telephoned the Psychic Hotline and was told, "You are going to meet a beautiful young woman who will want to know everything about you."

The frog said, "That's great! Will I meet her at a party, or what?"

"No," said the psychic, "Next term—in her biology class."

* * *

A man is caught sitting at a make-shift campfire by a forest ranger, and to the ranger's horror, the man is eating a bald eagle. The man is consequently put in jail for the crime. On the day of his trial, the conversation goes something like this:

JUDGE: "Do you know that eating a bald eagle is a federal offense?"

MAN: "Yes I do. But if you let me argue my case, I'll explain what happened."

JUDGE: "Proceed."

MAN: "I got lost in the woods. I hadn't had anything to eat for two weeks. I was so hungry. Next thing I see is a bald eagle swooping down at the lake for some fish. I knew that if I followed the eagle, I could maybe steal the fish. I caught up with the eagle who lighted upon a tree stump to eat the fish. I threw a stone toward the eagle hoping he would drop the fish and fly away. Unfortunately, in my weakened condition, my aim was off, and the rock hit the eagle squarely on his poor little head, and killed it. I thought long and hard about what had happened, but figured that since I killed it I might as well eat it since it would be more disgraceful to let it rot on the ground."

JUDGE: "The court will take a recess while I consider your testimony."

(15 minutes go by and the judge returns.)

JUDGE: "Due to the extreme circumstance you were under and because you didn't intend to kill the eagle, the court will dismiss the charges."

The Judge then leans over the bench and whispers: "If you don't mind my asking, what does a bald eagle taste like?"

MAN: "Well your honor, it's hard to explain. The best I can describe it is somewhere between a California condor and a spotted owl."

* * *

Muldoon lived alone in the Irish countryside with only a pet dog for company. One day the dog died, and Muldoon went to the parish priest and asked, "Father, me dog is dead. Could ya' be saying a mass for the poor creature?"

Father Patrick replied, "I'm afraid not; we cannot have services for an animal in the church. But there are some Baptists down the lane, and there's no tellin' what they believe. Maybe they'll do something for the creature."

Muldoon said, "I'll go right away, Father. Do ya' think $5,000 will be enough to donate for the service?"

Father Patrick exclaimed, "Holy Canine! Why didn't ya' tell me the dog was Catholic?"

* * *

A crafty old mountain lion used to hang around a ranch looking for stray cattle. One day he saw a bull off by himself and managed to kill it after a mighty battle. The bull was too heavy to drag off, so the mountain lion decided to just eat as much as he could hold. He ate and ate until he just couldn't eat any more. This made him feel really good, so he let out a big roar. That made him feel even better, so he roared again. He kept it up until the rancher came and shot him.

Moral: When you are full of bull, keep your mouth shut.

* * *

Some farmers were standing around shooting the breeze one day when the topic came around to animals and their distinguishing traits. The group agreed that the dog was probably the most loyal animal and the mule was undoubtedly the most stubborn.

Farmer Jones piped in, "You know, I believe probably the friendliest animal in all God's creation is the goose."

The others wanted to know how he arrived at such a conclusion. "Well," he explained, "I was out standing in my corn the other day, and a whole flock of 'em came by overhead. And, do you know, every single one of 'em honked and waved!"

* * *

Did you ever wonder why there are no dead penguins on the ice in Antarctica—where do they go? It is a known fact that the penguin is a very ritualistic bird which lives an extremely ordered and complex life. The penguin is very committed to its family and will mate for life, as well as maintaining a form of compassionate contact with its offspring throughout its life.

If a penguin is found dead on the ice surface, other members of the family and social circle have been known to dig holes in the ice, using their wings and beaks, until the hole is deep enough for the dead bird to be rolled into and buried. The male penguins then gather in a circle around the fresh grave and sing:

"Freeze a jolly good fellow"

"Freeze a jolly good fellow."

Then they kick him into the ice hole.

* * *

Two dogs were walking down the street. One dog said to the other, "Wait here a minute, I'll be right back." He walked across the street and sniffed a fire hydrant for about a minute, then walked back.

The other dog said, "What was that about?"

The first dog said, "I was just checking my messages."

* * *

Farmer Jones's cows stopped giving good milk. So he went around asking for advice, and someone told him that happy cows give good milk. So every morning he would go out and tell some jokes to his cows, and they would all laugh. But the rest of the cows in the community thought that the jokes were pretty stupid. Because of this, his cows became the laughing stock of the town.

* * *

My dog used to chase people on a bike a lot. It got so bad I had to take his bike away.

* * *

A burglar broke into a house one night. He shone his flashlight around, looking for valuables, and when he picked up a CD player to place in his sack, a strange, disembodied voice echoed from the dark saying, "Jesus is watching you." He nearly jumped out of his skin, clicked his flashlight out, and froze.

When he heard nothing more after a bit, he shook his head, clicked the light back on and began searching for more valuables. Just as he pulled the stereo out so he could disconnect the wires, clear as a bell he heard, "Jesus is watching you." Freaked out, he shone his light around frantically, looking for the source of the voice. Finally, in the corner of the room, his flashlight beam came to rest on a parrot.

"Did you say that?" he hissed at the parrot.

"Yep," the parrot confessed, "I'm just trying to warn you."

The burglar relaxed. "Warn me, huh? Who are you?"

"Moses," replied the bird.

"Moses!" the burglar laughed. "What kind of stupid people would name a parrot Moses?"

"Probably the same kind of people that would name a rottweiler Jesus," the bird answered.

* * *

The other day I was on my way home from work when the most remarkable thing happened. Traffic was heavy as usual, and as I sat at a red light, out of nowhere a bird slammed into my windshield. If that wasn't bad enough, the poor creature got its wing stuck under the windshield wiper.

Just then the light turned green and there I was with a bird stuck on my windshield. Without any other apparent options, turning on the windshield wipers seemed the only thing to do. It actually worked. On the upswing, the bird flew off, and here is the crazy thing: it slammed right onto the windshield of the car behind me. No, it didn't get caught under the windshield wipers of that vehicle, but the car behind me was a police car.

Of course, immediately the lights went on and I was forced to pull over. The officer walked up and told me he saw what had happened at the light. Trying to plead my case fell on deaf ears. He simply stated, "I'm going to have to write you up for flipping me the bird."

* * *

A grasshopper walked into a bar. The bartender said, "Hey, we have a drink named after you."

The grasshopper said, "You have a drink named Larry?"

* * *

Two robins were sitting in a tree. "I'm really hungry," said the first one.

"Me, too," said the second. "Let's fly down and find some lunch."

They flew to the ground and found a nice plot of plowed ground full of worms. They ate and ate and ate and ate until they could eat no more. "I'm so full I don't think I can fly back up to the tree," said the first one.

"Me neither. Let's just lie here and bask in the warm sun," said the second.

"OK," said the first. So they plopped down, basking in the sun.

No sooner had they fallen asleep than a big fat tomcat snuck up and gobbled them up.

As he sat washing his face after his meal, he thought, "I love baskin' robins."

* * *

A man's dog goes missing and he is frantic. His wife says, "Why don't you put an ad in the paper?"

He does, but two weeks later the dog is still missing. "What did you put in the paper?" his wife asks.

"Here boy!" he replies.

* * *

A Russian scientist and a Czech scientist had spent their whole lives studying the majestic grizzly bear. Each year they petitioned their respective governments to allow them to go to Yellowstone to study these wondrous beasts.

Finally, their request was granted and they immediately flew to New York and then on west to Yellowstone. They reported in to the local ranger station and were told that it was the grizzly mating season and it was much too dangerous to go out and study the animals.

They pleaded that this was their only chance. Finally the ranger relented. The Russian and the Czech were given cell phones and told to report in every day. For several days they called in, and then nothing was heard from the two scientists. The rangers mounted a search party and found the scientists' camp completely ravaged. There was no sign of the missing men.

They then followed the trail of a male and a female bear. They found the female and decided they must kill the animal to find out if she had eaten the scientists because they feared an international incident.

They killed the female and cut open the bear's stomach, where they found the remains of the Russian. One ranger turned to the other and said, "You know what this means, don't you?"

"Of course," the other ranger nodded. "The Czech is in the male."

* * *

There is a beautiful white bear in the zoo who, some days, is very playful and friendly, and other days he just lies in a dark corner and doesn't move. He's a bipolar bear.

* * *

A dog owner had a pit bull that hated to walk. He kept sitting down and bracing his feet so that his owner would have to drag him by his leash. The owner finally gave up when he realized that he was creating a bottomless pit!

* * *

Two rabbits were being chased by a pack of wolves. The wolves chased the rabbits into a thicket. After a few minutes, one rabbit turned to the other and said, "Well, do you want to make a run for it or stay here a few days and out-number them?"

* * *

A snail goes to the Datsun dealer and wants to order a new 280Z. The salesman says, "Sure, what color?"

The snail says, "Bright red, and instead of a 'Z' could you put an 'S' on it?"

The salesman says, "Sure," and the car is ordered. When the car comes in and the snail comes to pick it up, it's perfect — red and a 240S. The snail jumps in and roars off in a cloud of dust. The salesman turns to his buddy and says, "Wow! Look at that escargot!!"

* * *

Two boll weevils grew up in South Carolina. One went to Hollywood and became a famous actor. The other stayed behind in the cotton fields and never amounted to much. The second one, naturally, became known as the lesser of two weevils.

* * *

A jogger running down a country road was startled as a horse yelled at him, "Hey! Come over here, buddy!"

The jogger was stunned but ran over to the fence where the horse was standing and asked, "Were you talking to me?"

The horse replied, "Sure was. Man, I've got a problem. I won the Kentucky Derby a few years ago and this stupid farmer bought me. Now all I do is pull a plow, and I'm sick of it. Why don't you run up to the house and offer him $5,000 to buy me. I'll make you some money cause I can still run."

Dollar signs appeared in the jogger's head. So he ran to the house and found the old farmer sitting on the porch. The jogger yelled to the farmer, "Hey, old man, I'll give you $5,000 for that broken-down old nag you've got in the field."

The farmer replied, "Son, this has happened before. You can't believe anything that horse says. He's never even been to Kentucky."

* * *

Three nature lovers wanted to take pictures of bears for their photo album, so one day they went for a drive in the mountains. They drove along an old dirt road until they entered the trees. As they rounded a curve, they spotted a sign that read, "BEAR LEFT."

So they turned around and went home.

* * *

While sports fishing off the Florida coast, a tourist capsized his boat. He could swim, but his fear of alligators kept him clinging to the overturned craft. Spotting an old beachcomber standing on the shore, the tourist shouted, "Are there any gators around here?!"

"Naw," the man hollered back, "they ain't been around for years!"

Feeling safe, the tourist started swimming leisurely toward the shore. About halfway there he asked the guy, "How'd you get rid of the gators?"

"We didn't do nothin'," the beachcomber said. "The sharks got 'em."

* * *

A rich man was trying to find his daughter a birthday gift when he saw a poor man with a beautiful white horse. He told the man that he would give him $500 for the horse. The poor man replied, "I don't know mister, it don't look so good," and walked away.

The next day the rich man came back and offered the poor man $1000 for the horse. The poor man said, "I don't know mister, it don't look so good."

On the third day the rich man offered the poor man $2000 for the horse, and said he wouldn't take no for an answer. The poor man agreed, and the rich man took the horse home. The rich man's daughter loved her present. She climbed onto the horse, then galloped right into a tree. The rich man rushed back over to the poor man's house, demanding an explanation for the horse's blindness.

The poor man replied, "I told you it don't look so good."

*   *   *

A lady was walking down the street to work and saw a parrot in a pet store. She stopped to admire the bird. The parrot said to her, "Hey lady, you are really ugly."

The lady was furious! She stormed past the store to work. On the way home she saw the same parrot in the window and the parrot again said, "Hey lady, you are really ugly."

She was incredibly ticked now. The next day on the way to work she saw the same parrot and once again it said, "Hey lady, you are really ugly."

The lady was so furious that she stormed into the store and threatened to sue the store and have the bird killed. The store manager apologized profusely and promised the bird wouldn't say it again.

The next day, when the lady walked past the store after work the parrot said to her, "Hey lady."

She paused, scowled with an icy and deadly stare, and said with a hoarse voice, "Yes?"

The bird, strutting back and forth on its perch in a cocky manner, said, "You know."

*   *   *

A man was driving along a highway and saw a rabbit jump out across the middle of the road. He swerved to avoid hitting it, but unfortunately the rabbit jumped right in front of the car. The driver, a sensitive man and animal lover, pulled over and got out to see what happened to the rabbit. Much to his dismay, the rabbit was dead. The driver felt so awful that he began to cry.

A beautiful blonde driving down the highway saw the man crying on the side of the road and stopped. She stepped out of the car and asked the man what was wrong. "I feel terrible," he said. "I accidentally hit this rabbit and killed it."

The blonde said, "Don't worry." She ran to her car and pulled out a spray can. She went over to the limp, dead rabbit, bent down, and sprayed the contents onto the rabbit. The rabbit jumped up, waved its paw at the two of them and hopped off down the road. Ten feet away the rabbit stopped, turned around and waved again, then he hopped down the road another ten feet, turned and waved, hopped another ten feet, turned and waved, and repeated this again and again and again, until he hopped out of sight.

The man was astonished. He ran over to the woman and demanded, "What did you spray on that rabbit?"

The blonde turned the can around so the man could read the label. It said, "Hair Spray—Restores life to dead hair, adds permanent wave."

*　　*　　*

During the Revolutionary War, there was a small encampment of Patriot soldiers in the woods. Before they went to bed that night, they tied chickens in the trees around the encampment. Sure enough, some British soldiers came stumbling through the woods in the night and frightened the chickens. Their squawks and clucks woke the Patriots and they were able to capture the entire group of British soldiers.

A few nights later, the cook prepared the chickens for dinner. The soldiers said, "This is really good. What do you call it?"

The chef said that in honor of these special chickens who saved their lives, he called it "Chicken Catch a Tory."

*　　*　　*

A Drug Enforcement officer stopped at a ranch in Montana and talked with an old rancher. He said, "I need to inspect your ranch for illegally grown drugs."

The old rancher said, "Okay, but don't go in that field over there," pointing out the location.

The agent exploded, saying, "Mister, I have the authority of the federal government with me." Reaching into his rear pants pocket, he removed his badge and proudly displayed it to the farmer. "See this badge? This badge means I am allowed to go wherever I wish, on any land. No questions asked or answers given. Have I made myself clear? Do you understand?"

The old rancher nodded politely, apologized, and went about his chores. A short time later, the old rancher heard loud screams and saw the DEA officer running for his life, chased close behind by the rancher's prize bull. With every step, the bull was gaining ground on the officer, and it seemed likely that he would get "horned" before he could reach safety. The officer was clearly terrified.

The old rancher threw down his tools, ran to the fence, and yelled at the top of his lungs, "Your badge! Show him your badge!"

* * *

A fly was buzzing along one morning when he saw a lawn mower someone had left out in their front yard. He flew over and sat on the handle, watching the children going down the sidewalk on their way to school. One little boy tripped on a crack and fell, spilling his lunch on the sidewalk. When he got up, he missed a piece of bologna. The fly had not eaten that morning, so he flew down and started eating the bologna. In fact he ate so much that he could not fly, so he waddled across the sidewalk, across the lawn, up the wheel of the lawn mower, up the handle, and sat there resting and watching the children.

There was still some bologna lying there on the sidewalk. He was really stuffed, but that baloney sure did look good. Finally temptation got the best of him and he jumped off the handle of the lawn mower to fly over to the baloney. But alas he was too full to fly and he went splat, killing himself instantly.

The moral of the story: Don't fly off the handle when you are full of baloney.

* * *

A city man took a winter vacation in an isolated rural area. After a few days of pure peace and quiet, though, he started to get restless. "What do you do for fun and excitement here?" he asked one of the locals.

"We go down to the lake and watch the moose dance on the ice," was the reply. "It's delightful."

The city fellow didn't think too much of that idea, but after another night of watching the wallpaper, he decided it was better than nothing. So that evening he went down to the lake. The next day he saw the local man who had recommended the trip. "I went down to the lake last night to watch the moose dance on the ice," the city man said. "It was the worst thing I ever saw. Those animals were so clumsy and uncoordinated, they were falling all over themselves."

"Well of course they were," snorted the local. "Nobody goes to the lake on Wednesday. That's amateur night."

* * *

A seafood restaurant had a sign in the window that read, "Big Lobster Tales, $5 each." Amazed at the great value, a man stopped in and asked the waitress, "Five dollars each for lobster tails—is that correct?"

"Yes," she said. "It's our special just for today."

"Well," he said, "they must be little lobster tails."

"No," she replied. "It's the really big lobster."

"Are you sure they aren't green lobster tails—and a little bit tough?"

"No," she said, "it's the really big red lobster."

"Big red lobster tails, $5 each?" he said, amazed. "They must be old lobster tails!"

"No, they're definitely today's."

"Today's big red lobster tails—$5 each?" he repeated, astounded.

"Yes," she insisted.

"Well, here's my five dollars," he said. "I'll take one."

She took the money and led him to a table where she invited him to sit down. She then sat down next to him, put her hand on his shoulder, leaned over close to him, and said, "Once upon a time there was a really big red lobster..."

* * *

A guy decided life would be more fun if he had a pet. So he went to the pet store and told the owner that he wanted to buy an unusual pet. After some discussion, he finally bought a talking centipede, which came in a little white box to use for its house. He took the box back home, found a good spot for it, and decided he would start off by taking his new pet to church with him.

So he asked the centipede in the box, "Would you like to go to church with me today? We will have a good time."

But there was no answer from his new pet. This bothered him a bit, but he waited a few minutes and then asked again, "How about going to church with me and receive a blessing?"

But again, there was no answer from his new friend and pet. So he waited a few minutes more, thinking about the situation. The guy decided to invite the centipede one last time.

This time he put his face up against the centipede's house and shouted, "Hey, in there! Would you like to go to church with me and learn about God?"

This time, a little voice came out of the box, "I heard you the first time! I'm putting my shoes on!"

* * *

Jon: I used to hunt grizzly bears with a club.

Bob: I don't believe that.

Jon: Why not?

Bob: Because it's too dangerous, hunting grizzly bears with a club.

Jon: Well, I don't do it anymore.

Bob: Why not?

Jon: The membership fees got too high.

* * *

After a talking sheepdog gets all the sheep into the pen, he reports back to the farmer, "All 40 accounted for."

"But I only have 36 sheep," says the farmer.

"I know," says the sheepdog. "But I rounded them up."

* * *

A dog had been deaf and blind for years. When she started to suffer painful tumors, it was time to put her down. When the father explained this to his seven-year-old son, the boy asked if Poochy would go to heaven. The father said he thought she would, and that in dog heaven, she would be healthy again and able to do her favorite thing: chase squirrels.

The boy thought about that for a minute, then said, "So dog heaven must be the same as squirrel hell."

* * *

A guy walked into a bar with a small dog. The bartender said, "Get out of here with that dog."

The guy said, "But this isn't just any dog. This dog can play the piano."

The bartender replied, "Well, if he can play that piano, you both can stay and have a drink on the house."

So the guy sat the dog on the piano stool, and the dog started playing. Ragtime, Mozart, Gershwin, and the bartender and all the patrons enjoyed the music.

Suddenly a bigger dog ran in, grabbed the small dog by the scruff of the neck, and dragged him out. The bartender asked the guy, "What was that all about?"

The guy replied, "Oh, that was his mother. She wanted him to be a doctor."

* * *

When a snail crossed the road, he was run over by a turtle. Regaining consciousness in the emergency room, he was asked what caused the accident. "I really can't remember," the snail said. "It all happened so fast."

* * *

A photographer had been trying for hours to get some action shots of a bear that preferred to sleep in its cage. "What kind of bear is that?" he finally asked the zookeeper.

"Himalayan," was the reply.

"I know that," said the photographer. "What I want to know is when him a getting up."

*   *   *

A lonely woman bought a parrot for companionship. After a week the parrot hadn't uttered a word, so the woman went back to the pet store and bought it a mirror. Nothing. The next week she brought home a little ladder. Polly was still uncommunicative, so the week after that, she gave it a swing, which elicited not a peep. A week later she found the parrot on the floor of its cage, dying. Summoning its last breath, the bird whispered, "Don't they have any food at that pet store?"

*   *   *

A man found a sheep wandering in his neighborhood and took it to the police station. The desk sergeant said, "Why don't you just take it to the zoo?"

The next day, the sergeant spotted the same guy walking down the street with the sheep. "I thought I told you to take that sheep to the zoo," he said.

"I know what you told me," the man replied. "Yesterday I took him to the zoo. Today I'm taking him to the movies."

*   *   *

A group of visitors to a national park were discussing recent bear sightings. "If you meet a bear, don't run," one person said.

His friend said, "Really? Why?"

The answer: "Bears like fast food."

*   *   *

Buffalo were roaming the range when a tourist passed by. "Those are the mangiest-looking beasts I've ever seen," he exclaimed.

One buffalo turned to another and said, "I think I just heard a discouraging word."

*   *   *

A guy walked into a bar with his golden retriever. "Hey, can I get a drink on the house if my dog talks for you?"

"Dogs can't talk, pal. But if you can prove to me yours does, I'll give you a drink. If not, you're going to get a beating."

"Okay." He turned to his dog. "Okay, fella. Tell me—what is on top of a house?"

"Roof!" The man turned and smiled at the bartender.

"THAT ain't talking! Any dog can bark!"

"Okay, boy. Tell me—how does sandpaper feel?"

"Ruff!"

"What are you tryin' to pull, mister?"

"Okay, okay," said the man. "One more question. Buddy, tell me—who is the greatest ball player who ever lived?"

"Ruth."

The bartender beat the guy up and threw him onto the sidewalk, then threw the dog out next to him. The dog stood up and looked at the guy.

"Wow. Maybe I shoulda said DiMaggio?"

*   *   *

A flock of sheep were romping in a meadow, happily going "baa baa" to each other and discussing life as usual, when suddenly they heard a "moo moooooooo!" They looked around and saw only sheep, so they carried on playing as before. Again, they heard "moo mooooooo!"

One of the sheep could hear it right next to him. He shuffled away from his friend, and asked, "Georgie, why are you mooing? You're a sheep. Sheep go 'baa'!"

His friend replied, "I know. I thought I would learn a foreign language!"

*   *   *

A man went to the vet with his goldfish. "I think it's got epilepsy," he told the vet.

The vet took a look and said, "It seems calm enough to me."

The man said, "Wait, I haven't taken it out of the bowl yet."

*   *   *

A cowboy was walking down the street with his new pet dachshund when a passerby asked him why in the world he would want such an "uncowboy-like" dog. He answered, "Somebody told me to get along little doggie."

*   *   *

"Yes, sir," panted the new shepherd, "I got all the sheep in, but I had to run some to get the lambs."

"Lambs, you idiot. Those 14 little ones are jack rabbits."

*   *   *

A breeder of fine horses saw this advertisement in a farm paper: "For five dollars, we will tell you how to cure horses of slobbering."

He sent in the five dollars and a few days later received the following information: "Teach him to spit."

*   *   *

Two small boys were petting their dogs and discussing the merits of each just like two farmers discuss the advantages of different breeds of livestock. One boy was from a family whose income allowed them to purchase a pure-bred dog. Trying to impress the poor boy, the wealthier one said, "We've got papers on our dog."

Knowing nothing about blood lines, the boy from the poor family replied, "Well, we've got papers *under* our dog."

*   *   *

One morning a man went out to feed his pet deer, but it wouldn't get up. He rushed into the house and brought something out and fed it to the deer. The deer got right up. A neighbor asked the man what he had fed the deer. He replied, "It was yeast to make my doe rise."

*   *   *

A nun was visiting a pet store and asked the manager if he had received any new pets for sale. He said that he had just gotten a new female parrot that very day. However, the parrot had been owned by a sailor and had horrible language—she cursed and uttered horrible oaths against anyone who came near. The nun said that wouldn't be a problem, since at the convent they had two parrots in a parrot room and they spent all their time praying. They would help clean up the language of the new parrot in no time.

So the nun bought the parrot and put her on a perch in the parrot room next to the other parrots, who were both male. Shortly after the nun left the room, one of the parrots turned to the other and said, "Hey, Jose, our prayers have been answered!"

* * *

Once upon a time there were two little skunks named "In" and "Out." They lived in a hollow tree with their mother. Sometimes In and Out played outside, but other times they played inside.

One day In was out and Out was in. The mother skunk asked Out to go out and bring In in. So Out went out and in a few minutes he came in with In.

"My, my, Out," she said, "how did you find In so quickly?"

Out just smiled and said, "Instinct."

* * *

Little Red Riding Hood was skipping down the road when she saw a big bad wolf crouched down behind a log. "My, what big eyes you have, Mr. Wolf." The wolf jumped up and ran away.

Farther down the road Little Red Riding Hood saw the wolf again and this time he was crouched behind a bush. "My, what big ears you have, Mr. Wolf," she said. Again the wolf jumped up and ran away.

About two miles down the road Little Red Riding Hood saw the wolf again and this time he was crouched down behind a rock. "My, what big teeth you have, Mr. Wolf."

With that the wolf jumped up and screamed, "Will you knock it off? I'm trying to poop!"

* * *

The reason the chicken crossed the road was to prove to the skunk that it could be done.

Age Is a Work of Art

A reporter asked Roger on his 100th birthday, "How do you account for your longevity?"

Roger replied, "You might call me a health nut. I've never smoked. I've never drunk alcohol. I was always in bed and sound asleep by 10:00 p.m. And I've always walked at least two miles a day, rain or shine."

The reporter said, "I had an uncle who followed that same routine and he died when he was 60. Why didn't it work for him?"

Roger said, "He didn't keep it up long enough."

* * *

A six-year-old went to the hospital with his grandma to visit his grandpa. When they got there, he ran ahead of his grandma and burst into his grandpa's room. "Grandpa, Grandpa," he said excitedly. "As soon as Grandma comes into the room, make a noise like a frog!"

"What?" said his grandpa.

"Make a noise like a frog, cause Grandma said that as soon as you croak, we're going to Disneyland!"

* * *

When I was younger, I hated going to weddings. After the wedding and during the reception, my aunts and the grandmotherly types would come up to me and poke me in the ribs, cackling, "You're next."

Finally they stopped, when I started doing the same to them at funerals!

* * *

Of course I talk to myself. Sometimes I need expert advice.

* * *

At my age, "getting lucky" means walking into a room and actually remembering what I came in there for.

* * *

I decided to stop calling the bathroom the "John" and renamed it the "Jim." I feel so much better saying I went to the Jim this morning.

* * *

At a prestigious dinner party, Christine announced, "My ancestry goes back all the way to Alexander the Great."

She then turned to Miriam and asked, "How far back does your family go?"

"I don't know," replied Miriam. "All of our records were lost in the flood."

* * *

Mabel was worried about an older woman, a widow, who lived in the apartment next door. She hadn't heard anything from her for a few days. So she told her son, "I want you to go next door and see how ol' Mrs. Jones is."

A few minutes later, the boy returned.

"Well, is she all right?" Mabel asked.

"She's fine, but she's annoyed with you," he said.

"At me? Whatever for?"

"Well," said her son, "Mrs. Jones told me it's none of your business how old she is."

* * *

When still a young man, Uncle Harry was told he would live a long life by adding a little gunpowder to his breakfast every morning. So every morning for the rest of his life he sprinkled some gunpowder on his morning eggs or corn flakes. The formula seemed to have worked as Uncle Harry lived to be 102 years old. At his death he left four children, 26 grandchildren, 58 great-grandchildren, 12 great-great-grandchildren, and a 15-foot hole in the side of the crematorium.

* * *

An older couple were lying in bed one night. The husband was falling asleep but the wife was in a romantic mood and wanted to talk. She said, "You used to hold my hand when we were courting." Wearily he reached across, held her hand for a second and tried to get back to sleep.

A few moments later she said, "Then you used to kiss me." Mildly irritated, he reached across, gave her a peck on the cheek and settled down to sleep.

Thirty seconds later she said, "Then you used to bite my neck."

Angrily, he threw back the bed clothes and got out of bed. "Where are you going?" she asked.

"To get my teeth!"

*   *   *

A man was telling his neighbor, "I just bought a new hearing aid. It cost me four thousand dollars, but it's state of the art."

"Really," answered the neighbor. "What kind is it?"

"Twelve-thirty."

*   *   *

An elderly couple had dinner at another couple's house, and after eating, the wives left the table and went into the kitchen. The two gentlemen were talking, and one said, "Last night we went out to a new restaurant and it was really great. I would recommend it very highly."

The other man said, "What is the name of the restaurant?"

The first man thought and thought and finally said, "What is the name of that flower you give to someone you love? You know . . . the one that is red and has thorns."

"Do you mean a rose?"

"Yes," the man said. He turned toward the kitchen and yelled, "Rose, what's the name of that restaurant we went to last night?"

*   *   *

An octogenarian who was an avid golfer moved to a new town and joined the local Country Club. He went to the Club for the first time to play but was told there wasn't anybody he could play with because they were already out on the course.

He repeated several times that he really wanted to play. Finally the Assistant Pro said he would play with him and would give him a 12-stroke handicap. The 80-year-old said, "I really don't need a handicap as I have been playing quite well. The only real problem I have is getting out of sand traps." And he did play well.

Coming onto the 18th the old man had a long drive, but it landed in one of the sand traps around the hole. Shooting from the sand trap he hit a very high ball which landed on the green and rolled into the hole!

The Pro walked over to the sand trap where his opponent was still standing. He said, "Nice shot, but I thought you said you have a problem getting out of sand traps?"

The octogenarian replied, "I do! Please give me a hand."

* * *

I think senility is going to be a fairly smooth transition for me.

* * *

One morning, a grandmother was surprised by her 7-year-old grandson, when he made her coffee. It was the worst cup of coffee in her life. When she got to the bottom, she found three little green army men in the cup. She said, "Honey, what are the army men doing in my coffee?"

Her grandson said, "Grandma, it says on TV: 'The best part of waking up is soldiers in your cup!'"

* * *

Adolph Hitler asked an astrologer, "On what day will I die?"

"You will die on a Jewish holiday" was the reply.

"How can you be so sure of that?" asked Hitler.

The astrologer said, "Any day you die will be a Jewish holiday."

* * *

A millionaire called a family conference. "I'm putting a box of money in the attic," he said. "When I die, I intend to grab it on my way up to heaven. See to it that no one touches it until it's my time to go."

The family respected his wishes. After his death the millionaire's wife looked in the attic. The box was still there. "The fool!" she said. "I *told* him he should have put it in the basement."

* * *

The rain was pouring down. And standing in front of a big puddle outside a pub was an old Irishman, drenched, holding a stick with a piece of string dangling in the water. A passer-by stopped and asked, "What are you doing?"

"Fishing," replied the old man.

Feeling sorry for the old man, the gent said, "Come in out of the rain and have a drink with me." In the warmth of the pub, as they sipped their drinks, the man could not resist asking, "So how many have you caught today?"

"You're the eighth," said the old man.

* * *

Three old men were discussing aging. "Sixty is the worst age to be," said the 60-year-old. "You always feel like you have to pee. And most of the time, you stand at the toilet and nothing comes out!"

"Ah, that's nothin'," said the 70-year-old. "When you're seventy, you don't have a bowel movement anymore. You take laxatives, eat bran, you sit on the toilet all day and nothin' comes out!"

"Actually," said the 80-year-old, "Eighty is the worst age of all."

"Do you have trouble peeing too?" asked the 60-year-old.

"No, not really. I pee every morning at 6:00. No problem at all."

"Do you have trouble having a bowel movement?"

"No, I have one every morning at 6:30."

With great exasperation, the 60-year-old said, "Let me get this straight. You pee every morning at 6:00 and have a bowel movement every morning at 6:30. So what's so tough about being 80?"

"I don't wake up until 7:00."

∗ ∗ ∗

A woman walked up to a little old man rocking in a chair on his porch. "I couldn't help noticing how happy you look," she said. "What's your secret for a long happy life?"

"I smoke three packs of cigarettes a day," he said. "I also drink a case of whiskey a week, eat fatty foods, and never exercise."

"That's amazing," the woman said. "How old are you?"

"Twenty-six," he said.

∗ ∗ ∗

How You Know When You're Marvelously Mature

1. You and your teeth don't sleep together.

2. Your try to straighten out the wrinkles in your socks and discover you aren't wearing any.

3. At the breakfast table you hear snap, crackle, pop and you're not eating cereal.

4. Your back goes out but you stay home.

5. Your idea of weight lifting is standing up.

6. You sit in a rocking chair and can't get it going.

7. The pharmacist has become your new best friend.

8. Getting "lucky" means you found your car in the parking lot.

9. You sink your teeth into a steak—and they stay there.

10. You wonder how you could be over the hill when you don't even remember being on top of it.

Doctor Please

A man was sitting at home one evening, when the doorbell rang. When he answered the door, a 6-foot tall cockroach was standing there. The cockroach immediately punched him between the eyes and scampered off.

The next evening, the man was sitting at home when the doorbell rang again. When he answered the door, the cockroach was there again. This time, it punched him, kicked him and karate chopped him before running away.

The third evening, the man was sitting at home when the doorbell rang. When he answered the door, the cockroach was there yet again. It leapt at him and stabbed him several times before running off. The gravely injured man managed to crawl to the telephone and summoned an ambulance. He was rushed to the emergency room, where they saved his life. The next morning, the doctor was doing his rounds. He asked the man what happened, so the man explained about the 6-foot cockroach's attacks, culminating in the near fatal stabbing.

The doctor thought for a moment and said, "Yes, there's a nasty bug going around."

* * *

An artist asked the gallery owner if there had been any interest in his paintings on display.

"I have good news and bad news," the owner replied. "The good news is that a gentleman inquired about your work and wondered if it would appreciate in value after your death. When I told him it would, he bought all 15 of your paintings."

"That's wonderful," the artist exclaimed. "What's the bad news?"

"The guy was your doctor."

* * *

Five doctors went duck hunting one day. Included in the group were a GP, a pediatrician, a psychiatrist, a surgeon and a pathologist. After a time, a bird came winging overhead. The first to react was the GP who raised his shotgun, but then hesitated.

"I'm not quite sure it's a duck," he said. "I think I'll have to get a second opinion." And of course by that time, the bird was long gone.

Another bird appeared in the sky. This time, the pediatrician drew a bead on it. He too, however, was unsure if it was really a duck in his sights and besides, it might have babies. "I'll have to do some more investigation," he muttered, as the creature made good its escape.

Next to see a bird flying was the sharp-eyed psychiatrist. Shotgun shouldered, he was more certain of his intended prey's identity.

"Now, I know it's a duck, but does it know it's a duck?" The fortunate bird disappeared while the fellow wrestled with this dilemma.

Finally, a fourth fowl sped past and this time the surgeon's weapon pointed skywards. BOOM!! The surgeon lowered his smoking gun and turned nonchalantly to the pathologist beside him.

"Go see if that was a duck, will you?"

* * *

A man walked into a doctor's office and said, "Doc, you have to help me. I think I'm a moth!"

The doctor said, "I can't help you. You need a psychiatrist. Why did you come in here?"

The man replied, "The light was on."

* * *

"Doctor," whined the patient. "I keep seeing spots before my eyes."

"Why have you come to me? Have you seen an ophthalmologist?"

"No," replied the patient, "just these spots."

* * *

The Hammetts were shown into the dentist's office, where Mr. Hammett made it clear he was in a big hurry.

"No expensive extras, Doctor," he ordered. "No gas or needles or any of that fancy stuff. Just pull the tooth and get it over with."

"I wish more of my patients were as stoic as you," said the dentist admiringly. "Now, which tooth is it?"

Mr. Hammett turned to his wife. "Show him your tooth, Honey."

* * *

Two little kids were in a hospital, lying on stretchers next to each other, outside the operating room. The first kid leaned over and asked, "What are you in here for?"

The second kid said, "I'm in here to get my tonsils out and I'm a little nervous."

The first kid said, "You've got nothing to worry about. I had that done when I was four. They put you to sleep, and when you wake up they give you lots of Jell-O and ice cream. It's a breeze!"

The second kid then asked, "What are you here for?"

The first kid said, "Circumcision."

And the second kid said, "Whoa! I had that done when I was born, and I couldn't walk for a year."

* * *

An exhausted looking man dragged himself in to his doctor's office. "Doctor Kaine, there are dogs all over my neighborhood. They bark all day and all night, and I can't get a wink of sleep."

"I have good news for you, Howard," Doctor Kaine said, rummaging through a drawer full of sample medications. "Here are some new sleeping pills that work like a dream. A few of these and your trouble will be over."

"Great," said Howard, "I'll try anything. Let's give it a shot."

A few weeks later Howard was back, looking worse than ever. "Doc, your plan is no good. I'm more tired than before!"

"I don't understand how that could be," said Dr. Kaine, shaking her head. "Those are the strongest pills on the market!"

"That may be true," answered Howard wearily, "but I'm still up all night chasing those dogs and when I finally catch one it's hard getting him to swallow the pill!"

* * *

I waited for my new doctor to make his way through the file that contained my very extensive medical history. After he finished all seventeen pages, he looked at me and said, "You look better in person than you do on paper."

* * *

During a visit to a mental hospital, a visitor asked the director what the criterion was which defined whether or not a patient should be institutionalized.

"Well," said the director, "we fill up a bathtub, then we offer a teaspoon, a teacup, and a bucket to the patient and ask him or her to empty the bathtub."

"Oh, I understand," said the visitor. "A normal person would use the bucket because it's bigger than the spoon or the teacup."

"Actually," said the director, "a normal person would just pull the plug. So tell me, do you want a room with an east view or a west view?"

* * *

The patient was adamant. "Doc, I need a liver transplant, a kidney transplant, a heart transplant, a cornea transplant, a spleen transplant, a pancreas trans . . ."

"What makes you think you need all those?"

"Well," replied the patient, "my boss said if I wanted to keep my job, I needed to get reorganized."

* * *

I was in the waiting room of my doctor's office the other day when the doctor started yelling, "Typhoid! Tetanus! Measles!"

I went up to the nurse and asked her what was going on. She told me that the doctor liked to call the shots around there.

* * *

A business executive injured his leg skiing one weekend. By the time he got home on Sunday, the leg was very swollen and he was having difficulty walking, so he called his physician at home. The doctor told him to soak it in hot water. He tried soaking it in hot water but the leg became more swollen and more painful.

His maid saw him limping and said, "I don't know, I'm only a maid, but I always thought it was better to use cold water, not hot, for swelling." He switched to cold water, and the swelling rapidly subsided.

On Monday morning he called his doctor again to complain. "Say Doc, what kind of a doctor are you anyway? You told me to soak my leg in hot water and it got worse. My maid told me to use cold water and it got better."

"Really?" answered the doctor. "I don't understand it. My maid said hot water."

* * *

The patient said, "It's been a month since my last visit and I still feel miserable."

His doctor replied, "Did you follow the instructions on the medicine I gave you?"

The patient said, "I sure did. The bottle said, 'Keep tightly closed.'"

* * *

A woman went to a doctor's office. She was seen by one of the new doctors, but after about 4 minutes in the examination room, she burst out, screaming as she ran down the hall. An older doctor stopped and asked her what the problem was, and she explained. He had her sit down and relax in another room.

The older doctor marched back to the first and demanded, "What's the matter with you? Mrs. Terry is 63 years old, she has four grown children and seven grandchildren, and you told her she's pregnant?"

The new doctor smiled smugly as he continued to write on his clipboard. "Cured her hiccups though, didn't it?"

* * *

I told my doctor that I broke my arm in two places. He told me to stop going to those places.

*   *   *

A man went to visit his doctor. "Doctor, my arm hurts bad. Could you check it out please?" the man pleaded.

The doctor rolled up the man's sleeve and suddenly heard the arm talk. "Hello, doctor. Could you lend me twenty bucks please? I'm desperate!" the arm said.

The doctor said, "Aha! I see the problem. Your arm is broke!"

*   *   *

Visiting a friend in the hospital, a woman noticed several pretty nurses who were wearing a pin that looked like an apple. She asked what the pin signified. A nurse replied, "Nothing. It's just to keep the doctors away."

*   *   *

A man said to his ophthalmologist, "Doc, I was looking in the mirror this morning, and I noticed that one of my eyes is different from the other!"

The doctor replied, "Which one?"

*   *   *

An X-ray technician asked a little girl, "Have you ever broken a bone?"

"Yes," she replied.

"Did it hurt?"

"No."

"Really? Which bone did you break?"

"My sister's arm."

*   *   *

Feeling listless, a woman bought some expensive "brain-stimulating" pills at the health-food store. But it wasn't until she got home that she read the label.

"This is just rosemary extract," she complained to her husband. "I can't believe that I spent all that money for something that I have growing wild in the yard."

"See?" he said. "You're smarter already."

* * *

A man rushed into the doctor's office and shouted, "Doctor! I think I'm shrinking!"

The doctor calmly responded, "Now, settle down. You'll just have to be a little patient."

* * *

A little old lady went to the doctor and said, "Doctor, I have this problem with gas, but it really doesn't bother me too much. They never smell and are always silent. As a matter of fact I've passed gas at least 20 times since I've been here in your office. You didn't know I was passing gas because they don't smell and are silent."

The doctor said, "I see. Take these pills and come back to see me next week."

The next week the lady went back. "Doctor," she said, "I don't know what the heck you gave me, but now when I pass gas although still silent they stink terribly."

"Good," the doctor said, "now that we've cleared up your sinuses, let's work on your hearing."

* * *

Doctor: "You have acute appendicitis."

Patient: "Oh, doctor, please don't flatter me."

* * *

I once went to a psychiatrist. He told me, "You're crazy."

I protested, "If you don't mind, I want a second opinion."

The psychiatrist said, "All right. You're ugly too."

* * *

A doctor said to his patient, "Let me put it this way, Mr. Smithers. The softness of your muscles is exceeded only by the hardness of your arteries."

* * *

Dr. Geezer & Dr. Young

An old physician, Doctor Gordon Geezer, became very bored in retirement and decided to re-open a medical clinic. He put up a sign outside that said: "Dr. Geezer's clinic. Get your treatment for $500—if not cured, get back $1,000."

Doctor Digger Young, who was positive that the old geezer didn't know beans about medicine, thought this would be a great opportunity to get $1,000. So he went to Dr. Geezer's clinic.

Dr. Young: "Dr. Geezer, I've lost all taste in my mouth. Can you please help me?"

Dr. Geezer: "Nurse, please bring medicine from box 22 and put 3 drops in Dr. Young's mouth."

Dr. Young: "Aaagh! This is gasoline!"

Dr. Geezer: "Congratulations! You've got your taste back. That will be $500."

Dr. Young was annoyed and went back after a couple of days, figuring to recover his money.

Dr. Young: "I've lost my memory. I can't remember anything."

Dr. Geezer: "Nurse, please bring medicine from box 22 and put 3 drops in the patient's mouth."

Dr. Young: "Oh, no you don't. That's gasoline!"

Dr. Geezer: "Congratulations! You've got your memory back. That will be $500."

Dr. Young left angrily and came back after several more days.

Dr. Young: "My eyesight has become weak—I can hardly see anything!"

Dr. Geezer: "Well, I don't have any medicine for that, so here's your $1000 back," and handed him a $10 bill.

Dr. Young: "But this is only $10!"

Dr. Geezer: "Congratulations! You got your vision back! That will be $500."

Love and Marriage

Shortly after a couple was married, the wife noticed that her husband was limping. She asked him why. He said that he'd been like that for years, and he didn't know why. She urged him to have a doctor check it out. He refused, and year after year, as she nagged him to get his limping taken care of, he steadfastly refused. Finally, after he retired, she finally prevailed on him to talk to a doctor about it. His doctor found that one of his legs was slightly longer than the other, and told him that the fix was simple and cheap. The husband said, "Let's do it," and within a few weeks he was walking without a limp and enjoying life as he never had before.

His wife immediately jumped all over him. "See," she said, "I told you to get that limp taken care of a long time ago."

He replied, "I stand corrected."

*   *   *

A woman walked into a store to return a pair of eyeglasses. The clerk asked, "What seems to be the problem?"

She replied, "I'm returning these glasses I bought for my husband. He's still not seeing things my way."

*   *   *

My wife thinks I put football before marriage, even though we just celebrated our third season together.

*   *   *

A guy said to his girlfriend, "I'd jump off a 500-foot cliff for you."

She replied, "Oh, that's just a big bluff."

*   *   *

My wife said, "Watcha doin' today?"

I said, "Nothing."

She said, "You did that yesterday."

I said, "I didn't finish."

*   *   *

A wife's definition of retirement: Twice as much husband on half as much pay.

*   *   *

A wife asked her husband, "Could you please go shopping for me and buy one carton of milk and if they have avocados, get 6."

A short time later the husband comes back with 6 cartons of milk. The wife asks him, "Why did you buy 6 cartons of milk?"

He replied, "Because they had avocados."

*   *   *

An elderly couple was celebrating their sixtieth anniversary. The couple had married as childhood sweethearts and had moved back to their old neighborhood after they retired. Holding hands, they walked back to their old school. It was not locked, so they entered and found the old desk they'd shared, where Jerry had carved "I love you, Sally." On their way back home, a bag of money fell out of an armored car, landing at their feet. Sally quickly picked it up and, not sure what to do with it, they took it home. There, she counted the money—fifty thousand dollars!

Jerry said, "We've got to give it back."

Sally said, "Finders keepers." She put the money back in the bag and hid it in the attic.

The next day, two police officers were canvassing the neighborhood looking for the money, and knocked on their door. "Pardon me, did either of you find a bag that fell out of an armored car yesterday?"

Sally said, "No."

Jerry said, "She's lying. She hid it up in the attic."

Sally said, "Don't believe him, he's getting senile."

The officers turned to Jerry and began to question him. "Tell us the story from the beginning."

Jerry said, "Well, when Sally and I were walking home from school yesterday . . ."

The first police officer turned to his partner and said, "We're outta here!"

* * *

After examining a woman who had been rushed to the Emergency Room, the doctor took the woman's husband aside and said, "I don't like the looks of your wife at all."

"Me neither, doc," said the husband. "But she's a great cook, and she's really good with the kids."

* * *

Earl and Bubba were quietly sitting in a boat fishing, chewing tobacco, and drinking iced tea, when suddenly Bubba said, "Think I'm gonna divorce the wife. She ain't spoke to me in over two months."

Earl spit overboard, took a long, slow sip of tea, and said, "Better think it over. Women like that are hard to find."

* * *

A bachelor is a man who prefers to go through life wanting something he doesn't have rather than having something he doesn't want.

* * *

The other day, my wife and I got into some petty argument. Neither of us would admit the possibility that we might be in error.

To her credit, she finally said, "Look. I'll tell you what. I'll admit I'm wrong if you admit I was right."

"Fine," I said.

She took a deep breath, looked me in the eye and said, "I'm wrong."

I grinned and replied, "You're right."

* * *

A mild-mannered man was reading a book on being self-assertive and decided to start at home. So he stormed into his house, pointed a finger in his wife's face, and said, "From now on I'm boss around here and my word is law! I want you to prepare me a gourmet meal and draw my bath. Then, when I've eaten and finished my bath, guess who's going to dress me and comb my hair?"

"The mortician," replied his wife.

*   *   *

A man and woman were married for many years. Whenever there was an argument, yelling could be heard deep into the night. The old man would shout, "When I die, I will dig my way up and out of the grave and come back and haunt you for the rest of your life!"

Neighbors feared him. The old man liked the fact that he was feared. Then one evening when he was 98, he died. After the burial, the woman's neighbors, concerned for her safety, asked, "Aren't you afraid that he may indeed be able to dig his way out of the grave and haunt you for the rest of your life?"

The wife said, "Let him dig. I had him buried upside down . . . and I know he won't ask for directions."

*   *   *

A married couple was asleep when the phone rang at two in the morning.

The wife picked up the phone, listened a moment, and said, "How should I know, that's 200 miles from here!" and hung up.

The husband said, "Who was that?"

The wife said, "I don't know. Some woman wanting to know if the coast is clear."

*   *   *

I married Miss Right. I just didn't know her first name was Always.

*   *   *

My husband bought me a mood ring the other day. When I'm in a good mood it turns green. When I'm in a bad mood, it leaves a red mark on his forehead.

* * *

Morris walks out into the street and manages to get a taxi just going by. He gets into the taxi, and the cabbie says, "Perfect timing. You're just like Dave."

"Who?"

"Dave Aronson. There's a guy who did everything right. Like my coming along when you needed a cab. It would have happened like that to Dave."

"There are always a few clouds over everybody," says Morris.

"Not Dave. He was a terrific athlete. He could have gone on the pro tour in tennis. He could golf with the pros. He sang like an opera baritone and danced like a Broadway star."

"He was something, huh?"

"He had a memory like a trap. Could remember everybody's birthday. He knew all about wine, which fork to eat with. He could fix anything. Not like me. I change a fuse, and I black out the whole neighborhood."

"No wonder you remember him."

"Well, I never actually met Dave."

"Then how do you know so much about him?" asks Morris.

"Because I married his widow."

* * *

I told my wife that I have the body of a Greek god.

She informed me that the Buddha was not Greek.

* * *

A man left work on Friday afternoon, but instead of going home, he stayed out the entire weekend hunting with the boys and spending his entire paycheck.

When he finally appeared at home Sunday night, he was confronted by his very angry wife and was barraged for nearly two hours with a tirade of his actions. Finally, his wife stopped the nagging and said to him. "How would you like it if you didn't see me for two or three days?"

To which he replied, "That would be fine with me."

Monday went by and he didn't see his wife. Tuesday and Wednesday came and went with the same results.

Thursday, the swelling went down just enough where he could see her a little out of the corner of his left eye.

* * *

Jesse and Mabel got married. On their honeymoon trip they were nearing Kansas City when Jesse put his hand on Mabel's knee. Giggling, she said, "Jesse, you can go a little farther now if you want to." So Jesse drove to Denver.

* * *

A guy and a girl were strolling across a pasture. The guy exclaimed, "Oh, look at that cow and the calf rubbing noses. That sight makes me want to do the same."

The girl said, "Well, go ahead. It's your cow."

* * *

Eight-year-old Sally brought her report card home from school. Her marks were good—mostly A's and a couple of B's. However, her teacher had written across the bottom: "Sally is a smart little girl, but she has one fault. She talks too much in school. I have an idea I'm going to try, which I think may break her of the habit."

Sally's dad signed her report card, adding a note on the back: "Please let me know if your idea works on Sally, because I would like to try it out on her mother."

* * *

Soon after their wedding, a lady's husband stopped wearing his wedding ring. She asked, "Why don't you wear your wedding band?"

He replied, "It cuts off my circulation."

She answered back, "It's supposed to!"

* * *

FOR SALE BY OWNER: Complete set of *Encyclopedia Britannica*. 45 volumes.

Excellent condition. $1,000.00 or best offer. No longer needed.

Got married last weekend. Wife knows everything.

* * *

A couple had been debating the purchase of a new vehicle for weeks. He wanted a new truck. She wanted a fast little sports car so she could zip through traffic around town.

He would probably have settled on any beat up old truck, but everything she seemed to like was way out of their price range.

"Look!" she said. "I want something that goes from 0 to 200 in 4 seconds or less. And my birthday is coming up. You could surprise me."

So for her birthday, he bought her a brand new bathroom scale.

* * *

A few minutes before the church service started, the people were sitting in their pews and talking. Suddenly, Satan appeared at the front of the church. Everyone started screaming and running for the exit, trampling each other in a frantic effort to get away from Evil incarnate. Soon everyone had left the church except for one elderly gentleman who sat calmly in his pew without moving, seemingly oblivious to the fact that the ultimate Enemy was in his presence.

So Satan walked up to the old man and said, "Don't you know who I am?"

The man replied, "Yep, sure do."

"Aren't you afraid of me?" Satan asked.

"Nope, sure ain't," said the man.

"Don't you realize I can kill you with a word?" asked Satan.

"Perhaps," returned the old man, in an even tone.

"Do you know that I can cause you profound, horrifying, physical agony?" persisted Satan.

"Probably," was the calm reply.

"And you're still not afraid?" asked Satan.

"Nope."

More than a little perturbed, Satan asked, "Well, why aren't you afraid of me?"

The man calmly replied, "Been married to your sister for over 45 years."

* * *

An Amish boy and his father were visiting a mall for the first time. They were amazed by almost everything they saw, but absolutely fascinated by the two shiny, silver walls that could move apart and back together again. The boy asked his father, "What is this, father?"

The father (never having seen an elevator) responded, "Son, I have never seen anything like this in my life. I don't know what it is." While the boy and his father were watching wide-eyed, an old lady in a wheel chair rolled up to the moving walls and pressed a button to the side of them.

The walls opened and the lady rolled between them and into a small room. The walls closed and the boy and his father watched small circles of light with numbers above the wall light up. They continued to watch the circles light up in the reverse direction. The walls opened up again and a beautiful 24-year-old woman stepped out. The father said to his son, "Go get your Mother!"

* * *

One day a man decided to wash his sweat-shirt. Seconds after he stepped into the laundry room, he shouted to his wife, "What setting do I use on the washing machine?"

"It depends," she replied. "What does it say on your shirt?"

He yelled back, "University of Oklahoma."

* * *

A young lady came home from a date, rather sad. She told her mother, "Anthony proposed to me an hour ago."

"Then why are you so sad?" her mother asked.

"Because he also told me he is an atheist. Mom, he doesn't even believe there's a Hell."

Her mother replied, "Marry him anyway. Between the two of us, we'll show him how wrong he is."

*   *   *

A devoted wife had spent her lifetime taking care of her husband. Now he had been slipping in and out of a coma for several months, yet she stayed by his bedside every single day. When he came to his senses, he motioned for her to come near him.

As she sat by him, he said, "You know what? You have been with me all through the bad times. When I got fired, you were there to support me. When my business failed, you were there. When I got shot, you were by my side. When we lost the house, you gave me support. When my health started failing, you were still by my side. You know what?"

"What dear?" she asks gently.

"I think you bring me bad luck."

*   *   *

Whenever a certain man went to a local discount store to get oil and filters for his car, he would buy his wife a bouquet of flowers on display near the checkout counter.

During one trip, some women in line behind him were "oohing" and "aahing" about a husband getting flowers for his wife. "How often do you do that?" one asked.

Before he could answer, the cashier, familiar with his routine, said, "Every three months or 3,000 miles, whichever comes first."

*   *   *

A couple were going out for the evening. They'd gotten ready, all dolled up, and put the cat out. The taxi arrived, and as the couple walked out of the house, the cat shot back in. They didn't want the cat shut in the house, so the wife went out to the taxi while the husband went upstairs to chase the cat out.

The wife, not wanting it known that the house would be empty, explained to the taxi driver, "He's just going upstairs to say good bye to my mother."

A few minutes later, the husband got into the cab. "Sorry I took so long," he said. "Stupid old thing was hiding under the bed and I had to poke her with a coat hanger to get her to come out!"

*   *   *

After a quarrel, a wife said to her husband, "You know, I was a fool when I married you."

The husband replied, "Yes, dear, but I was in love and didn't notice it."

*   *   *

The couple have not been getting along for years, so the husband thinks, "I'll buy my wife a cemetery plot for her birthday."

Well, you can imagine her disappointment. The next year, her birthday rolls around again and he doesn't get her anything.

She says, "Why didn't you get me a birthday present?"

He says, "You didn't use what I got you last year!"

*   *   *

An elderly Irishman lay dying in his bed. While suffering the agonies of impending death, he suddenly smelled the aroma of his favorite chocolate chip cookies wafting up the stairs. He gathered his remaining strength and lifted himself from the bed. Leaning against the wall, he slowly made his way out of the bedroom, and with even greater effort, gripping the railing with both hands, he crawled downstairs.

With labored breath, he leaned against the door frame, gazing into the kitchen. Were it not for death's agony, he would have thought himself already in heaven, for there, spread out upon waxed paper on the kitchen table were literally hundreds of his favorite chocolate chip cookies.

Was it heaven? Or was it one final act of heroic love from his devoted Irish wife of sixty years, seeing to it that he left this world a happy man? Mustering one great final effort, he threw himself towards the table, landing on his knees in a rumpled posture. His parched lips parted, the wondrous taste of the cookie was already in his mouth, seemingly bringing him back to life. The aged and withered hand trembled on its way to a cookie at the edge of the table, when it was suddenly smacked with a spatula by his wife . . .

"Hands off!" she said, "they're for the funeral."

* * *

An old man went to the Wizard to ask him if he could remove a curse he had been living with for 40 years.

The Wizard said, "Maybe, but you will have to tell me the exact words that were used to put the curse on you."

The old man said, "I now pronounce you man and wife."

* * *

I married my wife for her looks, but not the ones she's been giving me lately!

* * *

Farmer Jake had a nagging wife who made his life miserable. The only real peace that he got was when he was out in the field plowing. One day Jake's wife brought his lunch out to him. Then she stayed while he quietly ate and she berated him with a constant stream of nagging and complaining. Suddenly, Jake's old mule kicked up his back legs, striking the wife in the head, and killed her instantly.

At the wake, Jake's minister noticed that when the women offered their sympathy to Jake he would nod his head up and down. But when the men came up and spoke quietly to him, he would shake his head from side to side.

When the wake was over and all the mourners had left, the minister approached Jake and asked, "Why was it that you nodded your head up and down to all the women and shook your head from side to side to all the men?"

"Well," Jake replied, "The women all said how nice she looked, and her dress was so pretty, so I agreed by nodding my head up and down. The men all asked, 'Is that mule for sale!?'"

* * *

A guy said, "For our twentieth anniversary, I'm taking my wife to Australia."

His friend said, "That's going to be tough to beat. What are you going to do for your twenty-fifth anniversary?"

The first guy said, "I'm going to go back and get her."

*   *   *

Marvin found the following ransom note slipped under his front door. "Bring $50,000 to the 17th hole of your country club tomorrow at 10:00 a.m. if you ever want to see your wife alive again."

But it was well after 1:00 p.m. by the time he arrived at the designated meeting spot.

A masked man stepped out from behind a bush and demanded, "You're three hours late. What took you so long?"

"Give me a break!" said Marvin, pointing to his scorecard. "I'm a 27 handicap."

*   *   *

A little girl asked her mother, "How did the human race come about?"

The mother answered, "God made Adam and Eve and they had children and so all mankind was made."

Two days later she asked her father the same question. He said, "Many years ago there were monkeys, and we developed from them."

The confused girl returned to her mother and said, "Mom, how is it possible that you told me that the human race was created by God and Dad says we developed from monkeys?"

The mother answered, "Well dear, it is very simple. I told you about the origin of my side of the family, and your father told you about the origin of his side of the family."

*   *   *

After Adam stayed out late a few nights, Eve became suspicious. "You're running around with another woman. Admit it!" she demanded.

"What other woman?" Adam shot back. "You're it!"

That night, Adam was fast asleep when he was awakened by Eve poking him in the chest. "What are you doing?"

"Counting your ribs."

*   *   *

A woman awoke excitedly on Valentine's Day and announced enthusiastically to her husband, "I just dreamed that you gave me a diamond necklace for Valentine's day! What do you think it means?"

With certainty in his voice, the man said, "You'll know tonight." That evening the man came home with a small package and handed it to his wife.

With anxious anticipation the woman quickly opened the package to find a book titled *The Meaning of Dreams*.

*   *   *

The man was in no shape to drive, so he wisely left his car parked and walked home. As he was walking unsteadily along, he was stopped by a policeman.

"What are you doing out here at 2 a.m.?" asked the officer.

"I'm going to a lecture," the man said.

"And who is going to give a lecture at this hour?" the cop asked.

"My wife," said the man.

*   *   *

At a posh dinner party, a Latin American visitor was telling the guests about his home country and himself. As he concluded, he said, "And I have a charming and understanding wife but, alas, no children."

As his listeners appeared to be waiting for him to continue, he said, haltingly, "You see, my wife is unbearable."

Puzzled glances prompted him to try to clarify the matter: "What I mean is, my wife is inconceivable."

As his companions seemed amused, he floundered deeper into the intricacies of the English language, explaining triumphantly, "That is, my wife, she is impregnable!"

* * *

Girl: "I can't be your valentine for medical reasons."

Guy: "Really?"

Girl: "Yeah, you make me sick!"

* * *

A girl said to a friend, "I've been asked to get married lots of times."

The friend asked, "Who asked you?"

The girl said, "My mother and father."

* * *

My wife made me join a bridge club. I jump off next Tuesday.

* * *

A marriage counselor was asking a woman questions about her state of mind. "Did you wake up grumpy this morning?"

She said, "No, I let him sleep."

* * *

After 30 years of marriage, a couple was lying in bed one evening, when the wife felt her husband begin to fondle her in ways he hadn't in quite some time. It almost tickled as his fingers started at her neck, and then began moving down past the small of her back. He then caressed her shoulders and neck, slowly worked his hand down her front, stopping just over her lower stomach.

He then proceeded to place his hand on her left inner arm, caressed down her side again, passed gently over her buttock and down her leg to her calf. Then, he proceeded up her inner thigh, stopping just at the uppermost portion of her leg. He continued in the same manner on her right side.

Then he suddenly stopped, rolled over and started to watch the television. As she had become quite aroused by this caressing, she asked in a loving voice, "That was wonderful, dear. Why did you stop?"

He said, "I found the remote."

* * *

A drunk walked into a cafe. After staring at a beautiful woman for ten minutes, he walked over and kissed her. She jumped up and slapped him. "I'm sorry," he said. "I thought you were my wife. You look just like her."

"Ugh. Get away from me, you worthless, insufferable, no-good drunk!" she yelled.

"Wow, you even sound like her," he said.

* * *

My wife thinks I'm too nosy. At least that's what she keeps scribbling in her diary.

* * *

"Every once in a while my wife puts on one of those mud packs."

"Does it improve her looks?"

"Only for a few days—then the mud falls off."

* * *

"Why did you get rid of your waterbed?"

"Bill and I were drifting apart."

* * *

A tornado hit a farmhouse just before dawn one morning. It took the roof off, lifted up the beds on which the farmer and his wife slept, and set them down gently in the next county. The wife began to cry. The husband said, "Don't be scared, Mary. We're not hurt."

Mary said, "I'm not scared. I'm happy, because this is the first time in 14 years we've been out together."

* * *

Mom is driving her little girl to her friend's house for a play date. "Mommy," the girl asks, "how old are you?"

"Honey, you are not supposed to ask a lady her age," the mother warns. "It is not polite."

"OK," the little girl says. "How much do you weigh?"

"Now really," the mother says, "these are personal questions and are really none of your business."

Undaunted, the little girl asks, "Why did you and daddy get a divorce?"

"Those are enough questions, honestly!" The exasperated mother walks away as the two friends begin to play.

"My Mom wouldn't tell me anything," the little girl says to her friend.

"Well," said the friend, "all you need to do is look at her driver's license. It's like a report card. It has everything on it."

Later that night the little girl says to her mother, "I know how old you are. You are 32."

The mother is surprised and asks, "How did you find that out?"

"I also know that you weigh 140 pounds."

The mother is past surprise and shock now. "How in heaven's name did you find that out?"

"And," the little girl says triumphantly, "I know why you and daddy got a divorce."

"Oh really?" the mother asks. "Why?"

"Because you got an F in sex."

*   *   *

A man and his wife were having some problems at home and were giving each other the silent treatment. Suddenly, the man realized that the next day, he would need his wife to wake him at 5:00 a.m. for an early morning business flight. Not wanting to be the first to break the silence, he wrote on a piece of paper, "Please wake me at 5:00 a.m." He left it where he knew she would find it.

The next morning, the man woke up, only to discover it was 9:00 a.m. and he had missed his flight. Furious, he was about to go and see why his wife hadn't awakened him, when he noticed a piece of paper by the bed. The paper said, "It is 5:00 a.m. Wake up."

* * *

Several men are in the locker room of a golf club. A cell phone on a bench rings and a man engages the speaker function and begins to talk. Everyone in the room stops to listen.

MAN: "Hello."

WOMAN: "Honey, it's me. Are you at the club?"

MAN: "Yes."

WOMAN: "I'm at the mall now and found this beautiful leather coat. It's only $1,000. Is it OK if I buy it?"

MAN: "Sure, go ahead if you like it that much."

WOMAN: "I also stopped by the Mercedes dealership and looked at the new models. I saw one I really liked."

MAN: "How much?"

WOMAN: "$60,000."

MAN: "OK, but for that price I want it with all the options."

WOMAN: "Great! Oh, and one more thing . . . The house we wanted last year is back on the market. They're asking $950,000."

MAN: "Well, go ahead and give them an offer, but only $900,000."

WOMAN: "OK. I'll see you later! I love you!"

MAN: "Bye, I love you, too."

The man hangs up. The other men in the locker room are looking at him in astonishment. Then he asks, "Anyone know who this phone belongs to?"

* * *

An archeologist makes the best husband because the older his wife gets, the more interested he is.

* * *

A woman went to a lemon grove for a job and the foreman thought she was much too qualified. He said, "Do you even have any experience picking lemons?"

She said, "Yes, I've been divorced three times."

* * *

A husband and wife were reading quietly in bed when the wife looked over at him and asked, "What would you do if I died? Would you get married again?"

The husband said, "Definitely not!"

"Why not? Don't you like being married?"

He answered, "Of course I do."

"Then why wouldn't you remarry?"

"OK, OK, I'd get married again."

The wife said, "You would? . . . Would you live in our house?"

"Sure, it's a great house."

The wife asked, "Would you sleep with her in our bed?"

He said, "Where else would we sleep?"

"Would you let her drive my car?"

The husband answered, "Probably, it's almost new."

"Would you replace my pictures with hers?"

He said, "That would seem like the proper thing to do."

"Would you give her my jewelry?"

The husband replied, "No, I'm sure she'd want her own."

"Would she use my golf clubs?"

"No, she's left-handed." Whoops.

* * *

A redneck couple had 9 children. They went to the doctor to see about getting the husband "fixed." The doctor asked them why, after 9 children, they would choose to do this.

The husband replied that they had read that 1 out of every 10 children being born in the United States was Mexican and they didn't want a Mexican baby because neither of them could speak Spanish.

* * *

Love Poem:

My love, you take my breath away.

What have you stepped in to smell this way?

* * *

A mother was anxiously awaiting her daughter's plane. She had just come back from a faraway land where she was trying to find love and adventure.

As the daughter was exiting the plane, the mother noticed a man directly behind her. He was dressed in feathers with exotic markings all over his body and was carrying a shrunken head. The daughter introduced this man as her new husband.

The mother gasped in disbelief and screamed, "I said for you to marry a RICH doctor! A RICH doctor!"

* * *

A husband was coming out of anesthesia after surgery in a hospital. His wife was sitting at his bedside, when his eyes fluttered open and he murmured, "You're beautiful."

Flattered, the wife continued her vigil. Later the husband woke up again and said, "You're cute."

"What happened to beautiful?" asked the wife.

"The drugs are wearing off," the husband replied.

* * *

A man was known among his friends to be very brief and to the point; he never said much. One day, a saleswoman promoting a certain brand of cosmetics knocked on his door and asked to see his wife. The man told her that his wife wasn't home.

"Well," replied the saleswoman, "could I please wait for her?"

The man directed her to the living room and left her there for more than three hours. The saleswoman was getting worried, so she called out to the man in the other room and asked, "May I know where your wife is?"

"She went to the cemetery," he replied.

"And when is she returning?"

"I don't really know," he said. "She's been there eleven years now."

*　*　*

A man suddenly started feeling horrible and was sent to the hospital. The next day, the doctor had a talk with the man's wife. He said, "Your husband is suffering from serious stress. If immediate action is not taken, he could die in a very short time."

The woman said, "What type of immediate action?"

The doctor said, "You must provide a stress-free environment in your home. For the next month, make wonderful meals for him every day. Also, be sure that you don't nag him or stress him in any way."

On the drive home from the hospital, her husband asked, "So what's wrong with me, honey?"

The woman paused for a moment and then replied, "Sorry, honey, but you're going to die."

*　*　*

A little boy was in a relative's wedding. As he was coming down the aisle, he would take two steps, stop, turn to the crowd, put his hands up like claws and roar. So it went, step, step, ROAR, step, step, ROAR, all the way down the aisle. The crowd was near tears from laughing so hard by the time he reached the front. The little boy, however, was getting more and more distressed from all the laughing, and was near tears by the time he reached the front. When asked what he was doing, the child sniffed and said, "I was being the Ring Bear."

* * *

New husband: "Honey, I just got a notice from the bank saying we're overdrawn."

Newly-wed wife: "Try some other bank. They can't all be overdrawn."

* * *

Bob received a free ticket to the Super Bowl from his company. Unfortunately, when Bob arrived at the stadium he realized the seat was in the last row in the corner of the stadium. He was closer to the Goodyear Blimp than the field! About halfway through the first quarter, Bob noticed an empty seat 10 rows off the field on the 50-yard line. He decided to take a chance and made his way through the stadium and around the security guards to the empty seat. As he sat down, he asked the gentleman sitting next to him, "Excuse me, is anyone sitting here?"

The man said "No."

Very excited to be in such a great seat for the game, Bob said to the man next to him, "This is incredible! Who in their right mind would have a seat like this at the Super Bowl and not use it?"

The man replied, "Well, actually, the seat belongs to me. I was supposed to come with my wife, but she passed away. This is the first Super Bowl we haven't attended together since we got married in 1969."

"That's really sad," said Bob. "But still, couldn't you find someone to take the seat? A relative or a close friend?"

"No," the man replied, "they're all at the funeral."

* * *

Bill's barn burned down, and his wife Polly called the insurance company. She told them, "We had that barn insured for fifty thousand, and I want my money."

The agent replied, "Hold on just a minute, Polly. Insurance doesn't work quite like that. We will ascertain the value of what was insured and provide you with a new barn of comparable worth."

There was a long pause before Polly replied, "Then I'd like to cancel the policy on my husband."

* * *

Sarah was reading a newspaper, while her husband was engrossed in a magazine. Suddenly, she burst out laughing.

"Listen to this," she said. "There's a classified ad here where a guy is offering to swap his wife for a season ticket to the stadium."

"Hmmm," her husband said, not looking up from his magazine.

Teasing him, Sarah said, "Would you swap me for a season ticket?"

"Absolutely not," he said.

"How sweet," Sarah said. "Tell me why not."

"Season's more than half over," he said.

* * *

Fred and his wife Edna went to the state fair every year. Every year Fred would say, "Edna, I'd like to ride in that there airplane."

And every year Edna would say, "I know, Fred, but that airplane ride costs ten dollars, and ten dollars is ten dollars."

One year Fred and Edna went to the fair and Fred said, "Edna, I'm 71 years old. If I don't ride that airplane this year, I may never get another chance."

Edna replied, "Fred, that there airplane ride costs ten dollars, and ten dollars is ten dollars."

The pilot overheard them and said, "Folks, I'll make you a deal. I'll take you both up for a ride. If you can stay quiet for the entire ride and not say one word, I won't charge you, but if you say one word, it's ten dollars."

Fred and Edna agreed, and up they went. The pilot did all kinds of twists and turns, rolls and dives, but not a word was heard. He did all his tricks over again, but still not a word. They landed and the pilot turned to Fred. "By golly, I did everything I could think of to get you to yell out, but you didn't."

Fred replied, "Well, I was gonna say something when Edna fell out, but ten dollars is ten dollars."

* * *

The husband was sitting on the edge of the bed, observing his wife as she turned back and forth, looking at herself in the mirror. Since her birthday was not far off, he asked what she'd like to have for her birthday. "I'd like to be six again," she replied, still looking in the mirror.

On the morning of her birthday, he arose early, made her a big bowl of Lucky Charms, and then took her to Six Flags theme park. What a day! He put her on every ride in the park: the Death Slide, the Wall of Fear, the Screaming Monster Roller Coaster, every ride in the park. Five hours later they staggered out of the park. Her head was reeling and her stomach felt upside-down. He then took her to McDonald's where he ordered her a Happy Meal with extra fries and a chocolate shake. Then it was off to a movie, with popcorn, soda pop, and her favorite candy, M&M's. What a fabulous adventure! Finally she wobbled home with her husband and collapsed into bed exhausted.

He leaned over his wife with a big smile and lovingly asked, "Well dear, what was it like being six again?" Her eyes slowly opened and her expression suddenly changed. "I meant my dress size, you dummy!"

Moral of the story: Even when a man is listening, he's going to get it wrong.

* * *

A wife was in labor with her first child. Things were going well when suddenly she began to shout, "Shouldn't! Wouldn't! Couldn't! Can't!"

"Doctor, what's wrong with my wife!" her husband cried.

"It's perfectly normal," the doc reassured him. "She's just having her contractions."

* * *

A man and his wife were out playing golf when he hit a slice and ended up behind a big building. His wife said, "Look, both doors are open. If you can hit it through there with a little draw on it you could be pretty close to the green." He looked it over and decided to do it. He hit the ball, the ball hit the building, bounced back, hit his wife in the head and killed her on the spot.

A few years later, the man remarried, and was out playing golf with his new wife. He ended up in the same spot, behind the building. His new wife said, "Look, both doors are open. If you can hit it through there with a little draw on it you could be pretty close to the green."

The man said, "Oh no, I tried that once and took a double-bogie."

*   *   *

One day, after a man had his annual physical, the doctor came out and said, "You had a great check-up. Is there anything that you'd like to talk about or ask me?"

"Well," he said, "I was thinking about getting a vasectomy."

"That's a big decision! Have you talked it over with your family?"

"Yeah, we took a vote . . . and they're in favor of it 15 to 2."

*   *   *

A bookseller conducting a market survey asked a woman, "Which book has helped you most in your life?"

The woman replied, "My husband's check book!"

*   *   *

A pharmacist said to his customer, "Sir, please understand, to buy an anti-depressant you need a proper prescription. Simply showing a marriage certificate and your wife's picture is not enough!"

*   *   *

A wife said to her husband, "There's trouble with the car. It has water in the carburetor."

Her husband replied, "Water in the carburetor? That's ridiculous."

The wife said, "I tell you the car has water in the carburetor."

The husband said, "You don't even know what a carburetor is. I'll check it out. Where's the car?"

His wife replied, "In the pool."

* * *

A man told his friend he was getting married, and the friend said, "Have you picked a date yet?"

The man said, "Are you kidding? You can bring a date to your own wedding?"

* * *

A woman brought an old picture of her dead husband, wearing a hat, to the photographer. She wanted to know if the photographer could remove the hat from the picture. He convinced her he could easily do that, and asked her what side of his head he parted his hair on.

"I forget," she said. "But you can see that for yourself when you take off his hat."

* * *

Matt's dad picked him up from school to take him to a dental appointment. Knowing the parts for the school play were supposed to be posted that day, he asked his son if he got a part.

Matt enthusiastically announced that he'd gotten a part. "I play a man who's been married for twenty years."

"That's great, son. Keep up the good work and before you know it, they'll be giving you a speaking part."

* * *

An elderly couple were driving across the country. The woman was driving when she got pulled over by the highway patrol. The officer said, "Ma'am, did you know you were speeding?"

The woman turned to her husband and asked, "What did he say?" The old man yelled, "He says you were speeding!"

The patrolman said, "May I see your license?"

The woman turned to her husband and asked, "What did he say?" The old man yelled, "He wants to see your license!" The woman gave him her license.

The patrolman said, "I see you are from Arkansas. I spent some time there once and went on a blind date with the ugliest woman I've ever seen."

The woman turned to her husband and asked, "What did he say?"

The old man yelled, "He thinks he knows you!"

*   *   *

A young man excitedly told his mother that he'd fallen in love and was going to get married. He said, "Just for fun, Ma, I'm going to bring over three women and you try and guess which one I'm going to marry." The mother agreed.

The next day, he brought three beautiful women to the house and sat them down on the couch and they talked for a while. Later he said, "Okay, Ma, guess which one I'm going to marry."

She immediately replied, "The one in the middle."

"That's amazing, Ma. You're right. How did you know?"

"I don't like her."

*   *   *

When I first met my girlfriend, I said, "Can I ask you two questions?"

She said, "Of course. What's the second question?"

*   *   *

Men are like fine wine. They all start out like grapes, and it's women's job to stomp on them and keep them in the dark until they mature into something they'd like to have dinner with.

*   *   *

A mother was dropping her son off at a friend's house. She said to him, "Will you be good while Mommy's gone?"

The boy replied, "If you give me a dollar!"

His mother shook her head and said to him, "Why can't you be good for nothing like your father?!"

* * *

Guy: "Ever since we got married, my wife has tried to change me. She got me to stop drinking, smoking, running around at all hours of the night and more. She taught me how to dress well, enjoy the fine arts, gourmet cooking, classical music, and how to invest in the stock market."

Friend: "Sounds like you may be bitter because she spent so much time trying to change you."

Guy: "I'm not bitter. Now that I'm so improved, she just isn't good enough for me."

* * *

When Nancy found out she was pregnant, she told the good news to anyone who would listen. Her 4-year-old son overheard some of his mother's conversations. One day when Nancy and her son were shopping, a woman asked the little boy if he was excited about the new baby.

"Yes!" the 4-year-old said, "and I know what we're going to name it, too."

"Really?" asked the lady.

"Yes," said the little boy. "If it's a girl we're going to call her Christina, and if it's another boy we're going to call it quits!"

* * *

At a marriage seminar dealing with communication, the instructor stated, "It is essential that husbands and wives know the things that are important to each other." Addressing the men, he said, "Can you describe your wife's favorite flower?"

Tom leaned over to his wife Grace, touched her arm gently, and whispered, "It's Pillsbury All-Purpose, right?"

* * *

When Linda and Jim were dating, Linda became concerned over the lavish amount of money Jim was spending on her. After an expensive dinner date, she asked her mother, "What can I do to stop Jim from spending so much money on me?"

Her mother replied simply, "Marry him."

* * *

She was only a whiskey maker, but he loved her still.

* * *

Susie said to her boyfriend, "Todd, do you love me with all your heart?"

Todd said, "Yeah."

Susie said, "Do you think I'm the most beautiful girl in the world?"

Todd said, "Uh-huh."

Susie said, "Do you think my lips are like rose petals?"

Todd said, "Uh-huh."

Susie said, "Oh, you say the most wonderful things!"

* * *

I'd live life in the fast lane, but I'm married to a speed bump.

* * *

My husband and I divorced over religious differences. He thought he was God, and I didn't.

* * *

A man said to another, "My wife doesn't appreciate me. Does yours?"

The other one replied, "I wouldn't know. I've never heard her mention your name."

* * *

A wife said to her husband, "I baked two kinds of cookies today. Take your pick."

The husband replied, "No, thanks. I'll use my axe."

*   *   *

The bride said, "The two best things I cook are meat loaf and apple dumplings."

The groom said, "Which is this?"

*   *   *

A man walked into his house panting and exhausted. "What happened?" asked his wife.

"It's a great new idea I have," he gasped. "I ran all the way home behind the bus and saved a dollar."

"That wasn't very bright," she said. "Why didn't you run behind a taxi and save ten dollars?"

*   *   *

Leonard, an avant-garde painter, got married. Someone asked the bride a few months after the wedding, "How's married life, Susan?"

"It's great," she said. "My husband paints and I cook; then we try to guess what he painted and what I cooked."

*   *   *

A couple walking in the park noticed a younger man and woman sitting on a bench, kissing passionately. "Why don't you do that?" said the wife.

"Honey," replied her husband, "I don't even know that woman."

*   *   *

A woman told her friend, "I've finally found a way to get money out of my husband. We were arguing last night, and I told him I was going home to Mother. He gave me the bus fare."

*   *   *

My wife claims I'm a baseball fanatic. She says all I ever read about is baseball. All I ever talk about is baseball. All I ever think about is baseball. I told her she's way off base.

*   *   *

My wife asked if she could have a little peace and quiet while she cooked the dinner, so I took the batteries out of the smoke alarm.

* * *

Anyone got an owner's manual for a wife? Mine makes a terrible whining noise!

* * *

My wife apologized for the first time ever today. She said she's sorry she ever married me.

* * *

Discussing a friend's marriage that was on the rocks, a woman said that the problem was largely psychological. "He's psycho, and she's logical."

* * *

Halfway through dinner in a romantic restaurant, the husband smiled and said, "You look so beautiful under these lights." She swooned and felt she was falling in love again, until he added, "We gotta get some of these lights."

* * *

At a couple's 50th wedding anniversary party, someone remarked that they never seemed to fight. The husband said, "We battled, but it never amounted to much. After a while one of us always realized that I was wrong."

* * *

The bride wanted to play the violin at her own wedding reception, but as she tuned up, a string snapped. Her mother made the announcement to the guests: "I'm sorry to say that Paula cannot perform today. Her G string broke."

* * *

A woman spent the morning going to a beauty salon and then to a chiropractor. When she arrived home, she heard her husband, formerly an auto mechanic, talking on the phone. "She's not in. She's gone out for a paint job and a realignment."

* * *

Like a lot of husbands throughout history, Webster would sit down and try to talk to his wife. But as soon as he would start to say something, his wife would say, "And what's that supposed to mean?" Thus, *Webster's Dictionary* was born.

* * *

A man met his wife-to-be at a travel agency. She was looking for a vacation, and he was the last resort.

* * *

On their 25th wedding anniversary, a man took his wife out to dinner. Their teenage daughters said they'd have dessert waiting for them when they returned. After they got home, they saw that the dining table was beautifully set with china, crystal and candles, and there was a note that read: "Your dessert is in the refrigerator. We are staying with friends, so go ahead and do something we wouldn't do!"

"I suppose," the husband said, "we could vacuum."

* * *

Alex asked his wife where she wanted to go for their anniversary. She said, "Somewhere I haven't been in a long time!" So he suggested the kitchen.

* * *

A middle-aged woman said to her new boyfriend, "I'm a very good house-keeper. Each time I get a divorce, I keep the house."

* * *

An old guy who had spent endless hours at the corner tavern decided to mend his ways. "Wife," he said, "do you think you can forgive me my short-comings?"

"Husband," she replied, "it ain't so much your short-comings I've minded. It's your long-goings."

* * *

A real-estate agent was showing an old house to a woman who made a few sketches on a pad and admitted, "I could do a lot with that house." But then she added wistfully, "On the other hand, I believe I said the same thing the first time I looked at my husband."

*   *   *

A girl said to her boyfriend, "Whenever I look at you, I'm reminded of a famous man."

Her boyfriend said, "Really? Who?"

She said, "Darwin."

*   *   *

A girl said to her date, "Do you know why I won't marry you?"

The guy said, "I can't think."

The girl said, "You got it."

*   *   *

A girl said to her date, "Would you like to take a walk?"

He replied, "I'd love to."

She said, "Don't let me detain you."

*   *   *

A guy said to his friend, "I just had a date with a pair of Siamese twins."

His friend asked, "Did you have a good time?"

He said, "Yes and no."

*   *   *

Keith said to his friend, "This article says men become bald more often than women because of the heightened activity of their brains."

His friend replied, "Yes, and women don't grow beards because of the intense activity of their chins."

*   *   *

On a recent transatlantic flight, a plane passes through a severe storm. The turbulence is awful. Suddenly one wing is struck by lightning. A woman on the plane starts to lose it. She stands up in the front of the plane screaming, "I'm too young to die!" Then she yells, "Well, if I'm going to die, I want my last minutes to be memorable! Is there ANYONE on this plane who can make me feel like a WOMAN?"

For a moment there is silence. Everyone has forgotten their own peril. They all stare, riveted, at the desperate woman in the front of the plane.

Then a man stands up in the rear of the plane. "I can make you feel like a woman," he says. He is gorgeous, tall, muscular, with long, wavy black hair and jet black eyes.

He starts to walk slowly up the aisle, unbuttoning his shirt, one button at a time. No one moves.

He removes his shirt.

Muscles ripple across his chest. As he reaches her, he extends the arm holding his shirt out to the trembling woman, and says, "Iron this."

* * *

A married couple was celebrating their 50th wedding anniversary at a quiet, romantic little restaurant.

Suddenly, a tiny beautiful Fairy appeared on their table. She said, "For being such an exemplary married couple and especially for being so thoughtful and loving to each other for all this time, I will grant you each a wish."

"Oh," said the wife, "I want to travel around the world with my darling husband."

The fairy waved her magic wand, and—poof!—two tickets for a luxury liner and ten thousand dollars appeared in her hands. Then it was the husband's turn.

He thought for a minute and said, "Well, this is all very romantic, but an opportunity like this will never come again. I'm sorry my love, but my wish is to have a wife 20 years younger than me." The wife and the Fairy were shocked and disappointed. But a wish is a wish.

So, the Fairy waved her magic wand, and—poof!—the husband became 90 years old.

The Moral of the story: Men who are ungrateful husbands should remember: Fairies are female.

* * *

Men and Women:

A woman has the last word in any argument. Anything a man says after that is the beginning of a new argument.

A woman worries about the future until she gets a husband. A man never worries about the future until he gets a wife.

Men wake up as good-looking as they went to bed. Women somehow deteriorate during the night.

Any married man should forget his mistakes. There's no use in two people remembering the same thing.

Going to Church

Two boys were walking home from Sunday school after hearing strong preaching on the devil. One said to the other, "What do you think about all this Satan stuff?"

The other boy replied, "Well, you know how Santa Claus turned out. It's probably just your dad."

* * *

After the church service a little boy told the pastor, "When I grow up, I'm going to give you some money."

"Well, thank you," the pastor replied, "but why?"

"Because my daddy says you're one of the poorest preachers we've ever had."

* * *

A father was reading Bible stories to his young son. He read, "The man named Lot was warned to take his wife and flee out of the city, but his wife looked back and was turned to salt."

His son asked, "What happened to the flea?"

* * *

Gladys Dunn was new in town and decided to visit the church nearest to her new apartment. She appreciated the pretty sanctuary and the music by the choir, but the sermon was long and boring. Glancing around, she saw many in the congregation nodding off.

After the service, she turned to a still sleepy-looking gentleman next to her, extended her hand, and said, "I'm Gladys Dunn."

He replied, "You and me both!"

* * *

The minister began his pastoral prayer:

"Dear Lord," he said with arms extended and a rapturous look on his upturned face, "without you we are but dust . . ."

He would have continued, but at that moment one obedient little girl (who was listening carefully to the minister) leaned over to her mother and asked quite audibly in her shrill little girl voice, "Mommy, what is butt dust?"

*   *   *

"I hope you didn't take it personally, Reverend," an embarrassed woman said after a church service, "when my husband walked out during your sermon."

"I did find it rather disconcerting," the preacher replied.

"It's not a reflection on you, sir," insisted the churchgoer. "Ralph has been walking in his sleep ever since he was a child."

*   *   *

Lost on a rainy night, a nun stumbled across a monastery and requested shelter there. Fortunately, she was just in time for dinner and was treated to the best fish and chips she had ever tasted.

After dinner, she went into the kitchen to thank the chefs. She was met by two of the Brothers. The first one said, "Hello, I am Brother Michael, and this is Brother Charles."

"I'm very pleased to meet you," replied the nun. "I just wanted to thank you for a wonderful dinner. The fish and chips were the best I've ever had! Out of curiosity, who cooked what?"

Brother Charles replied, "Well, I'm the fish friar."

She turned to the other Brother and said, "Then you must be . . . ?"

"Yes, I'm the chip monk."

*   *   *

An archaeologist was digging in the Negev Desert in Israel and came upon a casket containing a mummy. After examining it, he called the curator of a prestigious natural-history museum. "I've just discovered a 3,000-year-old mummy of a man who died of heart failure!" the excited scientist exclaimed.

The curator replied, "Bring him in. We'll check it out."

A week later, the amazed curator called the archaeologist. "You were right about the mummy's age and cause of death. How in the world did you know?"

"Easy. There was a piece of papyrus in his hand that said, '10,000 Shekels on Goliath.'"

*   *   *

A priest, a preacher, and a rabbi in Tennessee used to get together two or three times a week for coffee and to talk about religion. One day, someone made the comment that preaching to people isn't really all that hard. A real challenge would be to preach to a bear.

One thing led to another and they decided to do an experiment. They would all go out into the woods, find a bear, preach to it, and attempt to convert it. Seven days later, they got together to discuss their experiences.

Father Flannery, who had his arm in a sling, was on crutches, and had various bandages, went first. "Well," he said, "I went into the woods to find me a bear. And when I found him I began to read to him from the Catechism. Well, that bear wanted nothing to do with me and began to slap me around. So I quickly grabbed my holy water, sprinkled him and, glory be, he became as gentle a lamb. The bishop is coming out next week to give him first communion and confirmation."

Reverend Billy Bob spoke next. He was in a wheelchair, with an arm and both legs in casts, and an IV drip. In his best oratory he claimed, "Well brothers, you know that we don't sprinkle! I went out and I found me a bear. And then I began to read to my bear from God's Holy Book. But that bear wanted nothing to do with me. So I took hold of him and we began to wrestle. We wrestled down one hill, up another and down another until we came to a creek. So I quick-like dunked him and baptized his hairy soul. And just like you said, he became as gentle as a lamb. We spent the rest of the week in fellowship, feasting on the Word, and praising the Lord."

They both looked down at the rabbi, who was lying in a hospital bed. He was in a body cast and traction with IV's and monitors running in and out of him. He was in bad shape. The rabbi looked up and said, "Looking back on it, I probably shouldn't have started with circumcision."

*   *   *

An elderly man took his little grandson for a walk around the local cemetery. Pausing before one gravestone, he said, "There lies a very honest man. He died owing me 50 dollars, but he struggled to the end to pay off his debts, and if anyone has gone to heaven, he has."

They walked on a bit farther and came to another grave. The old man pointed to the gravestone and said, "Now there's a different type of man altogether. He owed me 60 dollars, and he died without ever trying to pay me back. If anyone has gone to hell, he has."

The little boy thought for a while and then said, "You know, Grandpa, you are very lucky."

"Why?" asked the old man in surprise.

"Well, whichever place you go to, you'll have some money to draw on."

* * *

Little Susie, a six-year-old, came home from school whining, "Mommy, I've got a stomach ache."

"That's because your stomach is empty," her mother replied. "You'd feel better if you had something in it." She gave Susie a snack and sure enough, Susie felt better right away.

That afternoon the family's minister dropped by. While he was chatting with Susie's mom, he mentioned he'd had a bad headache all day long.

Susie perked up. "That's because it's empty," she said. "You'd feel better if you had something in it."

* * *

Ol' Fred was in the hospital near death, and the family called their preacher to be with them. As the Reverend stood next to the bed, Ol' Fred's condition appeared to deteriorate and he motioned frantically for something to write on. The pastor lovingly handed him a pen and a piece of paper, and Ol' Fred used his last bit of energy to scribble a note, then suddenly died.

The preacher thought it best not to look at the note at that time, so he placed it in his jacket pocket. At the funeral, as he was finishing the message, he realized that he was wearing the same jacket that he was wearing when Ol' Fred died.

He said, "You know, Ol' Fred handed me a note just before he died. I haven't looked at it, but knowing Fred, I'm sure there's a word of inspiration there for us all."

He opened the note and read, "Please step to your left—you're standing on my oxygen tube!"

*   *   *

It was Palm Sunday and, because of a sore throat, five-year-old Johnny stayed home from church with a sitter. When the family returned home, they were carrying several palm branches. The boy asked what they were for.

"People held them over Jesus' head as he walked by."

"Wouldn't you know it," the boy fumed. "The one Sunday I don't go, Jesus shows up!"

*   *   *

A paramedic was asked on a local TV talk-show, "What was your most unusual and challenging 911 call?"

"Recently we got a call from that big white church at 11th and Walnut," the paramedic said. "A frantic usher was very concerned that during the sermon an elderly man passed out in a pew and appeared to be dead. The usher could find no pulse and there was no noticeable breathing."

"What was so unusual and demanding about that particular call?" the interviewer asked.

"Well," the paramedic said, "we carried out four guys before we found the one who was dead."

*   *   *

A pastor went to the dentist for a set of false teeth. The first Sunday after he got his teeth, he preached for only eight minutes. The second Sunday, he talked for only ten minutes. The following Sunday, he talked for 2 hours and 48 minutes.

The congregation had to mob him to get him down from the pulpit, and they asked him what happened. The pastor explained the first Sunday his gums hurt so bad he couldn't talk for more than 8 minutes. The second Sunday his gums hurt too much to talk for more than 10 minutes. But, the third Sunday, by mistake he put his wife's teeth in and couldn't shut up.

*   *   *

Johnny's mother looked out the window and noticed him "playing church" with their cat. He had the cat sitting quietly and he was preaching to it. She smiled and went about her work.

A while later she heard loud meowing and hissing and ran back to the open window to see Johnny baptizing the cat in a tub of water. She called out, "Johnny, stop that! The cat is afraid of water!"

Johnny looked up at her and said, "He should have thought about that before he joined my church."

*   *   *

A preacher said, "Anyone with 'special needs' who wants to be prayed over, please come forward to the altar."

With that, Mulrooney got in line, and when it was his turn, the preacher asked, "Mulrooney, what do you want me to pray about for you?"

Mulrooney replied, "Preacher, I need you to pray for help with my hearing."

The preacher put one finger of one hand in Mulrooney's ear, placed his other hand on top of Mulrooney's head, and then prayed and prayed and prayed. He prayed to the Almighty for Mulrooney, and the whole congregation joined in with great enthusiasm.

After a few minutes, the preacher removed his hands, stood back and asked, "Mulrooney, how is your hearing now?"

Mulrooney answered, "I don't know. It ain't 'til next week!"

*   *   *

"I give up!" the little boy said while kneeling in prayer beside his bed. "Art doesn't listen to me at all."

"Art? Art who?" asked his bewildered mother.

"Art in heaven," said the boy.

* * *

A small town had three churches: Presbyterian, Methodist, and Baptist. All three had a serious problem with squirrels in the church. Each church in its own fashion had a meeting to deal with the problem.

The Presbyterians decided that it was predestined that squirrels be in the church and that they would just have to live with them.

The Methodists decided they should deal with the squirrels lovingly in the style of Wesley. They humanely trapped them and released them in a park at the edge of town. Within 3 days, they were all back in the church.

The Baptists had the best solution. They voted the squirrels in as members. Now they only see them at Christmas and Easter.

* * *

One Sunday morning, after attending church services in Hartford, Connecticut, Mark Twain said to Dr. Doane, the minister, "I enjoyed your services this morning, doctor. I welcomed it like an old friend. I have, you know, a book at home containing every word of it."

"You have not," said the indignant Dr. Doane.

"I have so," countered Twain.

"Then please send it to me. I'd very much like to see it."

"I'll send it," promised Twain, and the following day he sent Doane an unabridged dictionary.

* * *

In a small Texas town there was a nativity scene that showed great skill and talent had gone into creating it. But one small feature bothered some out-of-town visitors—the three wise men were wearing firemen's helmets. They questioned a local woman about the helmets. She said, "You Yankees must never read your Bibles!"

When they said they couldn't recall anything about firemen in the Bible, the woman whipped out her Bible and jabbed her finger at a passage. "See," she said, "it says right here, 'The three wise men came from afar.'"

* * *

After the revival had concluded, the three pastors were discussing the results with one another.

The Methodist minister said, "The revival worked out great for us! We gained 4 new families."

The Baptist preacher said, "We did better than that! We gained 6 new families."

The Presbyterian pastor said, "Well, we did even better than that! We got rid of our 10 biggest trouble-makers!"

* * *

A little boy was overheard praying, "Lord, if you can't make me a better boy, don't worry about it. I'm having a real good time like I am."

* * *

The Sunday School teacher was describing how Lot's wife looked back and turned into a pillar of salt. Little Billy interrupted, "My mommy looked back once while she was driving, and she turned into a telephone pole!"

* * *

My pastor friend put sanitary hot air hand dryers in the restrooms at his church and after two weeks took them out.

I asked him why, and he confessed that they worked fine, but when he went into the men's restroom, he saw a sign that read: "For a sample of this week's sermon, push the button."

* * *

There was once a small rural community—so small, in fact, that the only church in town was a small Baptist church whose pastor had to double up as the local barber to make ends meet. A man living in this small community had invested wisely and was enjoying his newfound comfort. He looked into the mirror one day as he was about to shave and said to himself, "I make enough money now that I don't have to shave myself. I'll go down to the barber and let him shave me from now on." So he did.

He walked into the barber shop and was told that the preacher/barber was out calling on shut-ins. The barber's wife, Grace, said, "I usually do the shaves anyway. Sit down and I'll shave you." So he did.

She shaved him and he asked, "How much do I owe you?"

"Twenty-five dollars," Grace replied. The man thought that was rather expensive and that he might have to get a shave every other day. Nonetheless, he paid Grace and went on his way.

The next day, he woke up and found his face to be just as smooth as the day before. No need for a shave today, he thought. The next day he awoke to find his face as smooth as a baby's bottom. Wow! he thought. It amazed him, as he normally would need to shave daily to keep his clean-shaven look.

On day 4, he woke up and his face was still as smooth as the minute after Grace had finished. Now, somewhat perplexed, the man went down to the barber shop to ask some questions. This particular day, the pastor was in, and the man asked him why his face was as smooth as it was the first day it was shaven.

The kind old pastor gently explained, "Friend, you were shaved by Grace, and once shaved, always shaved."

* * *

The church treasurer went to the pastor with the bad news that they couldn't make the mortgage payment or pay the utilities. So the pastor told his congregation on Sunday morning, "We need an extra-large offering this morning." Then he added, "We will honor the person who gives the largest offering by inviting him or her to pick out three hymns for the service."

To the pastor's delight, there was a one thousand dollar bill in the plate, which made him so excited he asked the big giver to identify himself immediately.

A quiet little lady sitting in the back corner stood, and the pastor invited her to the front. Telling her how generous her gift was, he also invited her to select three hymns. Her eyes brightened as she looked over the congregation, pointed to the three handsomest men in the sanctuary, and said, "I'll take him and him and him."

* * *

Did you hear they arrested the devil? They got him on possession.

* * *

A pastor asked his flock, "What would you like people to say when you're in your casket?"

One member said, "I'd like them to say I was a great family man."

Another said, "I'd like them to say I helped people."

A third said, "I'd like them to say, 'Look! I think he's moving!'"

* * *

A young woman wanted a small, casual wedding, so she asked her brother, a lay minister, to officiate. He had never performed a wedding ceremony before, so he asked his own pastor for advice.

"My sister has asked me to marry her," he said, "and I'm not sure what to do."

His pastor answered, "Try telling her you just want to be friends."

* * *

A man had an important meeting and couldn't find a parking spot. He said, "Lord, please take pity on me. If you find me a parking space, I promise to go to church every Sunday for the rest of my life and give up swearing."

Miraculously, a spot opened right in front of his building. The man looked up and said, "Never mind. I found one."

* * *

Adam bit the fruit and, feeling great shame, covered himself with a fig leaf. Eve, too, felt shame and covered herself with a fig leaf. Then she went behind some trees to try on a maple leaf, a sycamore, and an oak.

* * *

A Sunday School teacher was telling his class the parable of the Prodigal Son. After describing the rejoicing of the household over the return of the wayward son, he spoke about one who, in the midst of the festivities, failed to share in the jubilant spirit of the occasion. He asked, "Can anybody tell me who this was?"

Nine-year-old Victoria had been listening closely to the story. She waved her hand in the air. "I know!" she said. "It was the fatted calf."

* * *

Adam and Eve were naming animals. Adam saw a big creature with a horn on its face and said, "What shall we call this one?"

"Why don't we call it a rhinoceros"?

"But, why?"

"Because it looks more like a rhinoceros than anything we've seen so far."

* * *

An elderly man in Phoenix calls his son in New York and says, "I hate to ruin your day, but I have to tell you that your mother and I are divorcing. Forty-five years of misery is enough."

"Pop, what are you talking about?" the son screams.

"We can't stand the sight of each other any longer," the old man says. "We're sick of each other, and I'm sick of talking about this, so you call your sister in Chicago and tell her," and he hangs up.

Frantic, the son calls his sister, who explodes on the phone. "They're not getting divorced if I have anything to do about it," she shouts. "I'll take care of this."

She calls Phoenix immediately, and screams at the old man. "You are NOT getting divorced. Don't do a single thing until I get there. I'm calling my brother back, and we'll both be there tomorrow. Until then, don't do a thing, DO YOU HEAR ME?" and hangs up.

The old man hangs up his phone and turns to his wife.

"Okay," he says, "they're coming for Thanksgiving and paying their own fares. Now, what do we tell them for Christmas?"

* * *

A man appears at the Pearly Gates.

"Have you ever done anything of particular merit?" St. Peter asks.

"Well, I can think of one thing," the man offers. "Once, on a trip to the Grand Canyon, I came upon a gang of violent bikers who were threatening a young woman. I directed them to leave her alone, but they wouldn't listen. So I approached the largest and most heavily tattooed biker. I smacked him on the head, kicked his bike over, ripped out his nose ring and threw it on the ground, and told him, 'Leave her alone now or you'll answer to me.'"

St. Peter was impressed. "When did this happen?"

"Just a couple minutes ago."

*   *   *

We all know that 666 is the Number of the Beast. But did you know:

00666 - Zip code of the Beast

Route 666 - Highway of the Beast

666 F - Oven temperature for roast Beast

666k - Retirement plan of the Beast

DCLXVI - Roman numeral of The Beast

0.005015 - Reciprocal of the Beast

1010011010 - Binary number of The Beast

443556 - Square of the Beast

2.8235 - Log of the Beast

1.738E289 - Anti-log of the Beast

29A - Hexadecimal number of the Beast

666! - Factorial of the Beast

Windows 666 - Bill Gates' personal Beast

*   *   *

Church Bulletin Oddities

Bertha Belch, a missionary from Africa will be speaking tonight at Calvary Memorial Church in Racine. Come tonight and hear Bertha Belch all the way from Africa.

Miss Charlene Mason sang, "I will not pass this way again," giving obvious pleasure to the congregation.

Ladies, don't forget the rummage sale. It's a chance to get rid of those things not worth keeping around the house. Don't forget your husbands.

During the absence of our Pastor, we enjoyed the rare privilege of hearing a good sermon when J.F. Stubbs supplied our pulpit.

Don't let worry kill you off, let the Church help.

Irving Benson and Jessie Carter were married on October 24 in the church. So ends a friendship that began in their school days.

A bean supper will be held on Tuesday evening in the church hall. Music will follow.

The senior choir invites any member of the congregation who enjoys sinning to join the choir.

The church will host an evening of fine dining, superb entertainment, and gracious hostility.

Barbara remains in the hospital and needs blood donors for more transfusions. She is also having trouble sleeping and requests tapes of Pastor Nate's sermons.

Blondes Galore

A college blonde was sitting in her U.S. government class. The professor asked her if she knew what Roe vs. Wade was about.

She pondered the question, then finally said, "That was the decision George Washington had to make before he crossed the Delaware."

* * *

A blonde was bragging about her knowledge of state capitals. She proudly said, "Go ahead, ask me, I know all of them."

A friend said, "OK, what's the capital of Wisconsin?"

The blonde replied, "Oh, that's easy: W."

* * *

Tim was visiting his blonde friend Tammy, who had acquired two new dogs. He asked her what their names were.

Tammy said that one was named Rolex and the other was named Timex.

Tim said, "Whoever heard of someone naming dogs like that?"

Tammy answered, "They're watch dogs!"

* * *

How do you keep a blonde at home?

Build a circular driveway.

* * *

I saw a distraught young lady weeping beside her car. "Do you need some help?" I asked.

She replied, "I knew I should have replaced the battery in this remote door unlocker. Now I can't get into my car. Do you think they [pointing to a distant convenient store] would have a battery to fit this?"

"Hmmm, I dunno. Do you have an alarm too?" I asked. "No, just this remote thingy," she answered, handing it and the car keys to me.

As I took the key and manually unlocked the door, I said, "Why don't you drive over there and check about the battery . . . It's too far to walk."

* * *

A blonde was riding in a commercial airliner, and there was a loud noise from outside the plane. The captain came on the intercom and said, "Attention passengers, we just lost one of our engines, but don't worry, the other three engines will keep us up. But we'll arrive at our destination about an hour behind schedule."

Half an hour later, another loud noise sounded from outside the plane. The captain once again came on the intercom, "Attention passengers, do not be alarmed. We lost another engine, but the other two will still keep us flying. We will arrive at our destination about three hours late."

The blonde leaned over to the passenger next to her and said, "If those other two engines go out, we'll be up here forever."

* * *

Once upon a time there was a blonde who lived in Denver. She had long hair and blue eyes, and she was sick of all the blonde jokes. One day she decided to get a make-over, so she cut and dyed her hair, then went out and bought a new convertible.

She went driving north into Wyoming and then picked a country road until she came across a herd of sheep blocking the road. She stopped and called the sheepherder over. "That's a nice flock of sheep," she said.

"Well, thank you," said the shepherd.

"Tell you what. I have a proposition for you," said the woman.

"Okay," he replied.

"If I can guess the exact number of sheep in your flock, can I take one home?" asked the woman.

"Sure," said the sheepherder. So, the girl sat up and looked at the herd for a second and then said, "382."

"Wow," said the herder. "That is exactly right. Go ahead and pick out the sheep you want to take home."

So the woman, now feeling smarter than she ever had in her whole life, went and picked out a small spotted one and put it in her car. Upon watching this, the herder approached the woman and said, "Okay, now I have a proposition for you."

"What is it?" queried the Colorado woman.

"If I can guess the real color of your hair, can I have my dog back?"

*　*　*

A blonde decided to sell her vacuum cleaner, since all it was doing was gathering dust.

*　*　*

A blonde went to an appliance store sale and found a bargain. "I would like to buy this TV," she told the salesman.

"Sorry, we don't sell to blondes," he replied.

She hurried home and dyed her hair, then came back and again told the salesman, "I would like to buy this TV."

"Sorry, we don't sell to blondes," he replied.

"Nuts, he recognized me," she thought.

So she got a complete disguise: haircut and new color, new outfit, big sunglasses. Then she waited a few days before she again approached the salesman. "I would like to buy this TV."

"Sorry, we don't sell to blondes," he replied.

Frustrated, she exclaimed, "How do you know I'm a blonde?"

"Because that's a microwave," he said.

*　*　*

A very attractive blond woman came out of her house and went straight to her mailbox at the street. She opened it, then slammed it shut and stormed back into the house. A little later she came out of her house again, went to the mail box and again opened it, then slammed it shut again. Angrily, back into the house she went. Then again she came out, marched to the mail box, opened it and then slammed it harder than ever.

Puzzled by her actions, a neighbor asked her, "Is something wrong?"

She replied, "There certainly is! My stupid computer keeps saying, 'You've Got Mail.'"

* * *

A blonde went out for a walk. She came to a river and saw another blonde on the opposite bank. "Yoo-hoo!" she shouted. "How can I get to the other side?"

The second blonde looked up the river then down the river and yelled back, "You ARE on the other side."

* * *

A guy took his blonde girlfriend to her first football game. They had great seats right behind their team's bench. After the game, he asked her how she liked the experience.

"Oh, I really liked it," she replied, "especially the cute guys with all the big muscles. But I just couldn't understand why they were killing each other over 25 cents."

Dumbfounded, her date asked, "What do you mean?"

"Well, I saw them flip a coin and one team got it and then for the rest of the game, all they kept screaming was, 'Get the quarterback! Get the quarterback!'"

* * *

Becoming very frustrated with the attitude of a shopkeeper, a young blonde declared, "Well, then, maybe I'll just go out and catch my own alligator and get a pair of alligator shoes for free!"

The shopkeeper replied with a smile, "Well, little lady, why don't you go give it a try?"

The blonde headed off to the swamp, determined to catch an alligator. Later in the day, the shopkeeper was driving home and spotted the young woman standing waist deep in the murky water, shotgun in hand.

He saw a huge 9-foot gator swimming rapidly toward her. With lightning reflexes, the blond took aim, shot the creature, and hauled it up onto the slippery bank.

Nearby were 7 more dead gators all lying belly up. The shopkeeper watched in amazement as the blond struggled with the gator. Then, rolling her eyes, she screamed in frustration: "Nuts! This one's barefoot, too!"

* * *

A blonde was walking by a travel agency and noticed a sign in the window, "Cruise Special $99!!" So she went inside, laid her money on the counter and said, "I'd like the $99 cruise special, please."

The agent grabbed her, dragged her in the back room and tied her to a large inner tube, then dragged her out the back door and downhill to the river, where he pushed her in and sent her floating.

A second blonde came by a few minutes later, saw the sign, and went inside, laid her money on the counter, and asked for the $99 special. She too was tied to an inner tube and sent floating down the river. Drifting into stronger current, she eventually caught up with the first blonde. They floated side by side for a while before the first blonde asked, "Do they serve refreshments on this cruise?"

The second blonde replied, "They didn't last year."

* * *

Josh was helping Sally, a blonde, clean out the trunk of her car. Inside, he noticed a bag labeled "Emergency Repair Kit." Looking at it a little closer, he saw a stick of dynamite inside.

Thinking that was a bit strange, he asked Sally what it was for.

She said, "It's part of my emergency repair kit."

Josh said, "I can see that, but why?"

Sally replied, "In case I have a flat and need to blow up one of my tires."

*   *   *

A blind man and his guide dog went into a bar and found their way to a barstool. After ordering a drink and sitting there for a while, the blind guy yelled to the bartender, "Hey, you wanna hear a blonde joke?"

The whole bar immediately became absolutely quiet. In a deep voice, the woman next to him said, "Before you tell that joke, you should know something. The bartender is blonde, the bouncer is blonde, and I'm a 6' tall, 200 lb. blonde with a black belt in karate. What's more, the woman sitting next to me is blonde and she's a weightlifter. The lady to your right is a blonde and she's a pro wrestler. So, think about it seriously, Mister . . . You still wanna tell that joke?"

The blind guy thought for a moment and said, "Nah, not if I'm gonna have to explain it five times."

*   *   *

Why was the blonde staring at the can of orange juice?

Because it said concentrate.

*   *   *

A blonde was overweight, so her doctor put her on a special diet. "I want you to eat regularly for 2 days, then skip a day, and repeat this procedure for 2 weeks. The next time I see you, you'll have lost at least 5 pounds."

When the blonde returned, she shocked the doctor by having lost nearly 20 pounds. "Why, that's amazing!" the doctor said. "Did you follow my instructions?"

The blonde nodded. "I'll tell you though, I thought I was going to drop dead that third day."

"From hunger, you mean?" asked the doctor.

"No, from skipping."

*   *   *

A blonde replaced all the windows in her house with expensive, double-insulated energy efficient windows. Twelve months later she got a call from the contractor, complaining that the work had been finished for a year and she still hadn't paid.

The blonde replied, "Now don't try to pull a fast one on me. Just because I'm blonde doesn't mean that I'm automatically stupid. The salesman who sold me those windows told me that in one year they would pay for themselves."

*   *   *

The blonde joined Facebook and saw that her password had to be at least 8 characters long, so she chose: MickeyMinniePlutoHueyLouieDeweyDonaldGoofy.

*   *   *

She was so blonde that she took a ruler to bed to see how long she slept.

*   *   *

A blonde goes into a restaurant and notices there's a "peel and win" sticker on her coffee cup. So she peels it off and starts screaming, "I've won a motor home! I've won a motor home!"

The waitress says, "That's impossible. The biggest prize is a free lunch."

But the blonde keeps screaming, "I've won a motor home! I've won a motor home!"

Finally the manager comes over and says, "Ma'am, I'm sorry, but you're mistaken. You couldn't possibly have won a motor home because we didn't have that as a prize!"

The blonde says, "No, it's not a mistake. I've won a motor home!"

She hands the ticket to the manager and he reads, "Win a Bagel."

*   *   *

Bill and his wife Bambi lived on an isolated canyon road. One morning Bambi heard the radio announcer say, "According to the weather forecast, we're going to have an estimated 12-16 inches of snow today through tomorrow, so please park your cars on the even-numbered side of the street so the snow plows can get through." Bambi, being a good citizen, went out and moved her car to the even-numbered side of the road.

Three days later they had a second storm, and while they were eating break-fast, the announcer said, "We are expecting 8 to 12 more inches of snow today. Please park your car on the odd-numbered side of the street, so the snow plows can get through." Bambi again went out and moved her car to the odd-numbered side of the road.

Several days later while having breakfast again, the radio announcer said, "We are expecting up to 12 more inches of snow today, so please . . ." Just then the electric power went off.

Bambi was very upset, and with a worried look on her face she said, "Bill, honey, I don't know what to do. Which side of the street do you think I need to park on so the snow plow can get through today?"

Bill said, "Why don't we just leave it in the garage this time?"

* * *

A blonde was recently hired at an office. Her first task was to go out for coffee. Eager to do well her first day on the job, she grabbed a large thermos and hurried to a nearby coffee shop. She held up the thermos and the coffee shop worker quickly came over to take her order. She asked, "Is this big enough to hold six cups of coffee?" The coffee shop worker looked at the thermos and said, "Yeah. It looks like about six cups to me."

"Oh good!" the blonde sighed in relief. "Then give me two regular, two black, and two decaf."

* * *

A blonde and a redhead are watching the six o'clock news one evening. The redhead bets the blonde $50 that the man in the lead story, who is threat-ening to jump from a 40-story building, will jump. "I'll take that bet," the blonde replied.

A few minutes later, the newscaster breaks in to report that the man had, indeed, jumped from the building. The redhead, feeling sudden guilt for having bet on such an incident, turns to the blonde and tells her that she does not need to pay the $50.

"No, a bet's a bet," the blonde replies. "I owe you $50 dollars."

The redhead, feeling even more guilty, replies, "No, you don't understand. I saw the three o'clock edition, so I knew how it was going to turn out."

"That's okay," the blonde replies. "I saw it earlier too, but I didn't think he'd do it again."

*　*　*

A suburban gal called 911 on her cell phone to report that her car had been broken into at the mall. She was hysterical, sitting in her car, describing her desperate situation to the Sheriff's dispatcher. "They've stolen the stereo, the steering wheel, the brake pedal and even the accelerator!" the blonde cried.

The Police Department dispatcher said, "Stay calm, Ma'am. An officer is on the way."

A few minutes later, the deputy radioed in. "Disregard. She got in the back seat by mistake."

*　*　*

A man who'd just died was delivered to a local mortuary wearing an expensive, expertly tailored black suit. The female blonde mortician asked the deceased's wife how she would like the body dressed. She pointed out that the man did look good in the black suit he was already wearing. The widow, however, said that she always thought her husband looked his best in blue, and that she wanted him in a blue suit. She gave the blonde mortician a blank check and said, "I don't care what it costs, but please have my husband in a blue suit for the viewing."

The woman returned the next day for the wake. To her delight, she found her husband dressed in a gorgeous blue suit with a subtle chalk stripe. The suit fit him perfectly. She said to the mortician, "Whatever this cost, I'm very satisfied. You did an excellent job and I'm very grateful. How much did you spend?"

To her astonishment, the blonde mortician gave her back the original blank check. "There's no charge," she said.

"No, really, I must compensate you for the cost of that exquisite blue suit!" she said.

"Honestly, ma'am," the blonde said, "it cost nothing. You see, a deceased gentleman of about your husband's size was brought in shortly after you left yesterday, and he was wearing an attractive blue suit. I asked his wife if she minded him going to his grave wearing a black suit instead, and she said it made no difference as long as he looked nice. So I just switched the heads."

* * *

A blonde named Judy tried to sell her old car. She was having a lot of problems, because the car had 250,000 miles. One day, she told her problem to a friend at work. Her friend told her, "There is a possibility to make the car easier to sell, but it's not legal."

"That doesn't matter," replied Judy, "if only I can sell the car."

"Okay," her friend said. "Here is the address of a friend of mine. He owns a car repair shop. Tell him I sent you and he will turn the counter in your car back to 50,000 miles. Then it won't be a problem to sell your car anymore."

The following weekend, Judy made the trip to the mechanic. Two weeks later the friend asked her, "Did you sell your car?"

"No," replied Judi, "why should I? It only has 50,000 miles on it!"

* * *

One young lady told her friend, "Whenever I'm down in the dumps I buy myself a dress."

The friend said, "I've always wondered where you got them."

* * *

A blonde woman walked up to a house and asked the owner whether there was any work she could do to earn some money. The man said, "Sure. You can paint my porch." He told her that the paint and other materials she might need were in the garage. They agreed on a price of $50. The man's wife, inside the house, heard the conversation and said to her husband, "Does she realize that the porch goes all the way around the house?"

The man replied, "She should. She was standing on it."

A short time later, the blonde came to the door to collect her money. "You're finished already?" the man asked.

"Yes," the blonde said, "and I had paint left over, so I gave it two coats."

Impressed, the man reached into his pocket for the $50 and handed it to her.

"And by the way," the blonde added, "it's not a Porch, it's a Lexus."

*   *   *

Two blondes were working on a house. The one who was nailing down siding would reach into her nail pouch, pull out a nail and either toss it over her shoulder or nail it in. The other, figuring this was worth looking into, asked, "Why are you throwing those nails away?"

The first explained, "If I pull a nail out of my pouch and it's pointed toward me, I throw it away 'cause it's defective. If it's pointed toward the house, then I nail it in!"

The second blonde got completely upset and yelled, "You moron! The nails pointed toward you aren't defective! They're for the other side of the house!"

*   *   *

A blonde decided one day to show her husband that she was a resourceful wife. So while her husband was off at work, she painted several rooms in the house. Her husband arrived home at 5:30 and smelled fresh paint. He walked into the living room and found his wife lying on the floor in a pool of sweat. He noticed that she was wearing a ski jacket and a fur coat at the same time. He went over and asked her if she was all right.

She replied, "Yes."

He asked, "What are you doing?"

She said that she wanted to prove to him how resourceful she was by painting the house herself.

He then asked her, "Why do you have a ski jacket over a fur coat?"

She replied that the directions on the paint can said, "FOR BEST RESULTS, PUT ON TWO COATS."

*   *   *

Two blondes were on the Interstate driving to Disneyland, when they saw a sign that said Disneyland LEFT. They started crying and turned around and went home.

Problems Aplenty

A man stopped for gas on his way home from work. As he finished pumping the gas, he spilled some of it on his arm. He immediately grabbed a paper towel and wiped it off. Then he got back in his car and continued down the highway. Unfortunately, he was addicted to smoking and decided to light up, but he got the lighter too close to his arm and lit it on fire. Since he was by then in the middle of heavy traffic and there was no place to pull off, he rolled down his window and held his arm outside, hoping the rushing air would blow out the fire. It didn't work, but a policeman saw his predicament, got him stopped, pulled out a fire extinguisher, and put out the fire. Then he wrote him a ticket—for brandishing a fire arm.

*　*　*

After the christening of his baby brother in church, Johnny sobbed all the way home in the back seat of the car. His father asked him over and over what was wrong.

Finally, the boy said, "The preacher said he wanted us to be brought up in a Christian home, but I want to stay with you guys."

*　*　*

A mother was preparing pancakes for her sons—Kevin 5 and Ryan 3. The boys began to argue over who would get the first pancake.

Their mother saw the opportunity for a moral lesson. "If Jesus were sitting here, He would say, 'Let my brother have the first pancake, I can wait.'"

Kevin turned to his younger brother and said, "Ryan, you be Jesus!"

*　*　*

An old timer in the Ozarks wanted to visit his cousin on the other side of the mountain, so he hitched up his horse and buggy and got his little dog, and set off down his dirt road. However, he made a wrong turn and found himself on an Interstate highway. Before he could find an exit, a huge Cadillac came roaring over the hill behind him and crashed into his buggy and knocked everything and everyone into the ditch.

After the man recovered, a lawyer convinced him to sue the driver of the Cadillac for several million dollars. In court, the old guy was testifying about his injuries and what happened, when the defense attorney barked at him, "You told the investigating State Trooper that you were all right."

The buggy driver replied, "Well, if you'll just hold your horses, I'll tell you about that. You see, I was goin' down the road in my buggy with my little dog beside me, and that giant Cadilliac automobile came roarin' over the hill and smashed into my wagon, broke my horse's two hind laigs, throwed me in the ditch, and my little doggie right beside me."

The defense attorney immediately interrupted and yelled, "But you told the investigating Trooper that you were all right!"

"Listen, sonny, I'm tryin' to explain it to ya. You see, I was going down the hill, tryin' to find a place to turn off, when this here locomotive came smokin' up behind me, blowin' firey smokestacks, smashed my wagon to smithereens, broke my horse's two hind laigs, throwed me in the ditch, and my little doggie right beside me. And when that Highway Patrolman came roarin' up with his big lights a flashin', he walked over to my horse and saw how he was sufferin', took out his big six-gun, and ka-boom, shot my horse right between the eyes. Then he walked over to my little doggie, looked how busted up he was, and ka-boom!, shot him too. Then with that cannon still smokin' in my eyes, he said to me, 'Are you all right?'"

* * *

A French guy accidentally caused the gas range in his kitchen to explode. His neighbors have nicknamed him Linoleum Blownapart.

* * *

A guy gets shipwrecked. When he wakes up, he's on a beach.

The sand is dark red. He can't believe it. The sky is dark red. He walks around a bit and sees there is dark red grass, dark red birds and dark red fruit on the dark red trees. He's shocked when he finds that his skin is starting to turn dark red too.

"Oh no!!" he says. "I've been marooned!!"

* * *

A businessman was in a great deal of trouble. His business was failing, he had put everything he had into the business, he owed everybody—it was so bad he was even contemplating suicide. As a last resort he went to a priest and poured out his story of tears and woe.

When he had finished, the priest said, "Here's what I want you to do: Put a beach chair and your Bible in your car and drive down to the beach. Take the beach chair and the Bible to the water's edge, sit down in the beach chair, and put the Bible in your lap. Open the Bible; the wind will riffle the pages, but finally the open Bible will come to rest on a page. Look down at the page and read the first thing you see. That will be your answer; that will tell you what to do."

A year later the businessman went back to the priest and brought his wife and children with him. The man was in a new custom-tailored suit, his wife in a mink coat, the children shining. The businessman pulled an envelope stuffed with money out of his pocket, gave it to the priest as a donation in thanks for his advice.

The priest recognized the benefactor, and was curious. "You did as I suggested?" he asked.

"Absolutely," replied the businessman.

"You went to the beach?"

"Absolutely."

"You sat in a beach chair with the Bible in your lap?"

"Absolutely."

"You let the pages riffle until they stopped?"

"Absolutely."

"And what were the first words you saw?"

"Chapter 11."

*　*　*

I have a phobia of over-engineered buildings.

I have a complex complex complex.

* * *

Just because nobody complains doesn't mean all parachutes are perfect.

* * *

Del heard that his father, grandfather and great-grandfather had all walked on water on their 21st birthdays. So, on his 21st birthday, Del and his big brother Damon headed out to the lake. "If they did it, I can too!" he insisted.

When Del and Damon arrived at the lake, they rented a canoe and began paddling. When they got to the middle of the lake, Del stepped off the side of the boat . . . and nearly drowned.

Furious and embarrassed, he and Damon headed for home. When Del arrived back at the house, he asked his grandmother for an explanation. "Grandma, why can't I walk on water like my father, and his father, and his father before him?"

His sweet old grandmother took Del by the hand, looked into his eyes, and explained, "That's because your father, grandfather, and great-grandfather were born in January. You were born in July, dear."

* * *

One young mushroom complained to another, "I don't know why the girls don't like me. I'm really a fun guy."

* * *

An American, an Englishman, a Scotsman, an Irishman, a Latvian, a Chinese, a Japanese, a Kiwi, a Canuck, an Eskimo, a Fijian, a Turk, an Aussie, a Yank, an Egyptian, a Spaniard, a Mongolian, a Tibetan, a Pole, a Mexican, a Spaniard, a Greek, a Russian, an Estonian, a German, an Indian, an Italian, a Brazilian, a Kenyan, a South African, a Filipino, a Pakistani, a Korean, an Argentinean, a Lithuanian, a Dane, a Finn, a Swede, an Israeli, a Romanian, a Bulgarian, a Serb, a Czech, a Croat, and a Panamanian go to a fancy night club.

The bouncer says, "Sorry. I can't let you in without a Thai."

* * *

A drunk stumbles onto a baptismal service on Sunday afternoon down by the river. He proceeds to walk down into the water and stand next to the Preacher.

The minister turns and notices the old drunk and says, "Mister, are you ready to find Jesus?"

The drunk looks back and says, "Yess, Preacher, I sure am."

The minister then dunks the fellow under the water and pulls him right back up. "Have you found Jesus?" the preacher asks.

"Nooo, I didn't!" says the drunk.

The preacher then dunks him under for quite a bit longer, brings him up and says, "Now, brother, have you found Jesus?"

"Noooo, I did not, Reverrend."

The preacher in disgust holds the man under for at least 30 seconds this time, brings him out of the water and says in a harsh tone, "My good man, have you found Jesus yet?"

The old drunk wipes his eyes and says to the preacher, "Are you sure this is where he fell in?"

*   *   *

One day many years ago, a fisherman's wife blessed her husband with twin sons. They loved the children very much, but couldn't think of what to name their children. Finally, after several days, the fisherman said, "Let's not decide on names right now. If we wait a little while, the names will simply occur to us."

After several weeks had passed, the fisherman and his wife noticed a peculiar fact. When left alone, one of the boys would always turn towards the sea, while the other boy would face inland. No matter which way the parents positioned the children, the same child always faced the same direction. "Let's call the boys Towards and Away," suggested the fisherman. His wife agreed, and from that point on, the boys were simply known as Towards and Away.

The years passed and the lads grew tall and strong. The day came when the aging fisherman said to his sons, "Boys, it's time that you learned how to make a living from the sea." They provisioned their ship, said their goodbyes, and set sail for a three-month voyage.

The three months passed quickly for the fisherman's wife, yet the ship had not returned. Another three months passed, and still no ship.

Three whole years passed before the grieving woman saw a lone man walking towards her house. She recognized him as her husband. "My goodness! What has happened to my darling boys?" she cried.

The ragged fisherman began to tell his story:

"We were just barely one whole day out to sea when Towards hooked into a great fish. Towards fought long and hard, but the fish was more than his equal. For a whole week they wrestled upon the waves without either of them letting up. Eventually the great fish started to win the battle, and Towards was pulled over the side of our ship. He was swallowed whole, and we never saw either of them again."

"Oh dear, that must have been terrible! What a huge fish that must have been! What a horrible fish. What a horrible, horrible fish!"

"Yes, it was, but you should have seen the one that got Away!"

* * *

The past, the present, and the future walked into a bar. It was tense.

* * *

I just got hit by a rented car. It Hertz.

* * *

I went shopping for some camouflage trousers, but I couldn't find any.

* * *

A young man riding a moped noticed a new Lamborghini parked in front of a country store. He stopped to take a closer look. Since the door was unlocked, he slid behind the wheel to imagine himself driving the expensive car. In the midst of his fantasy, he heard the door open and felt a hand jerk him from the vehicle. "What do you think you're doing?" the owner yelled at him. "Get out of my car!"

The owner started the engine and roared out of town. About a mile down the road, he noticed the man on the moped following him. Suddenly the rider passed him at about 100 mph. When the moped reached the horizon, it turned around and whizzed back by him in the opposite direction.

"What does he think he's doing?" he muttered, as he slammed down the accelerator and sped up to about 90 mph. Within a few seconds, the moped passed him again at a blinding speed, and again turned around at the horizon. Amazed, the driver pulled over and decided to ask the rider how he could make a moped go so fast. This time, however, as the moped returned it crashed into the front of the Lamborghini and flipped the rider into a ditch at the side of the road.

The driver ran over and asked, "Are you all right?"

The rider sat up slowly, shook his head, and said, "I think so."

"Tell me, what did you have in that bike to make it go so fast?"

"Nothing," the rider spat. "My suspenders got caught in the door of your car."

* * *

In the great days of the British Empire a new Commanding Officer was sent to a remote African bush outpost to relieve the retiring Colonel. After welcoming his replacement and showing the usual courtesies (gin and tonic, cucumber sandwiches, etc.) decreed by protocol, the retiring colonel said, "You must meet my Adjutant, Captain Smithers. He's my right-hand man and is really the strength of this entire post. His talent and energy are simply boundless."

Smithers was summoned and introduced to the new CO, who was surprised to meet a hunchback, one-eyed, toothless, hairless, scabbed and pockmarked specimen of humanity, a particularly unattractive man less than three feet tall. "Captain Smithers, old man, tell your new CO a bit about yourself."

"Well, sir, I graduated with honors from Sandhurst, joined the regiment, won the Military Cross and Bar after three expeditions behind enemy lines, represented Great Britain in equestrian events, won a Silver Medal in the middleweight boxing division of the Olympics, and I have researched the history of . . ."

At which point the colonel interrupted, "Yes, yes, never mind that, Smithers, he can find all that in your file. Tell him about the day you told the witch doctor to go stuff himself."

* * *

A champion jockey is about to enter an important race on a new horse.

The horse's trainer meets him before the race and says, "All you have to remember with this horse is that every time you approach a jump, you have to shout, 'ALLLLEEE OOOP!' really loudly in the horse's ear. Providing you do that, you'll be fine."

The jockey thinks the trainer is mad but promises to shout the command.

The race begins and they approach the first hurdle. The jockey ignores the trainer's ridiculous advice and the horse crashes straight through the center of the jump. They carry on and approach the second hurdle.

The jockey, somewhat embarrassed, whispers, "Aleeee ooop" in the horse's ear. The same thing happens—the horse crashes straight through the center of the jump. At the third hurdle, the jockey thinks, "It's no good; I'll have to do it" and yells, "ALLLEEE OOOP!" really loudly.

Sure enough, the horse sails over the jump with no problems. This continues for the rest of the race, but due to the earlier problems, the horse only finishes third. The trainer is fuming and asks the jockey what went wrong.

The jockey replies, "Nothing is wrong with me—it's this bloody horse. What is he—deaf or something?"

The trainer replies, "Deaf?? DEAF?? He's not deaf—he's BLIND!"

* * *

Police were called to a daycare center after a toddler resisted a rest.

* * *

Three mischievous boys went to the zoo one day for an outing, since they had been at school all week. They decided to visit the elephant cage, but soon enough, they were picked up by a cop for causing a commotion. The officer hauled them off to security for questioning. The supervisor in charge asked them to give their names and tell what they were doing at the elephant cage.

The first boy innocently said, "My name is Gary, and I was just throwing peanuts into the elephant cage."

The second added, "My name is Larry, and all I was doing was throwing peanuts into the elephant cage."

The third boy was a little shaken up and said, "Well, my name is Peter, but my friends call me Peanuts."

* * *

A young girl who was writing a paper for school came to her father and asked, "Dad, what is the difference between anger and exasperation?"

The father replied, "It is mostly a matter of degree. Let me show you what I mean." With that the father went to the telephone and dialed a number at random. To the man who answered the phone, he said, "Hello, is Melvin there?"

The man answered, "There is no one living here named Melvin. Why don't you learn to look up numbers before you dial them?"

"See," said the father to his daughter. "That man was not a bit happy with our call. He was probably very busy with something and we annoyed him. Now watch." The father dialed the number again. "Hello, is Melvin there?" asked the father.

"Now look here!" came the heated reply. "You just called this number and I told you that there is no Melvin here! You've got a lot of nerve calling again!" The receiver slammed down hard.

The father turned to his daughter and said, "You see, that was anger. Now I'll show you what exasperation means." He dialed the same number, and when a violent voice roared, "Hello!" the father calmly said, "Hello, this is Melvin. Have there been any calls for me?"

* * *

A film crew was on location deep in the desert. One day an old Indian went up to the director and said, "Tomorrow rain."

The next day it rained. A week later, the Indian went up to the director and said, "Tomorrow storm."

The next day there was a hailstorm. "This Indian is incredible," said the director. He told his secretary to hire the Indian to predict the weather for the remaining of the shoot. However, after several successful predictions, the old Indian didn't show up for two weeks.

Finally the director sent for him. "I have to shoot a big scene tomorrow," said the director, "and I'm depending on you. What will the weather be like?"

The Indian shrugged his shoulders. "Don't know," he said. "My radio is broken."

* * *

A man walked into Joe's Barber Shop for his regular haircut. As he snipped away, Joe asked, "What's up?"

The man explained that he was taking a vacation to Rome.

"Rome?!" Joe said. "Why would you want to go there? It's a crowded dirty city full of Italians! You'd be crazy to go to Rome! So how ya getting there?"

"We're taking JetBlue," the man replied.

"JetBlue?!" yelled Joe. "They're a terrible airline. Their planes are old, their flight attendants are ugly, and they're always late! So where you staying in Rome?"

The man said, "We'll be at the downtown International Marriot."

"That dump?!" said Joe. "That's the worst hotel in the city! The rooms are small, the service is surly and slow, and they're overpriced! So whatcha doing when you get there?"

The man said, "We're going to go see the Vatican and hope to see the Pope."

"Ha! That's rich!" laughed Joe. "You and a million other people trying to see him. He'll look the size of an ant. Boy, good luck on this trip. You're going to need it!"

A month later, the man came in for his regular haircut. Joe said, "Well, how did that trip to Rome turn out? Betcha JetBlue gave you the worst flight of your life!"

"No, quite the opposite," explained the man. "Not only were we on time in one of their brand new planes, but it was full and they bumped us up to first class. The food and wine were wonderful, and I had a beautiful 28-year-old flight attendant who waited on me hand and foot!"

"Hmmm," Joe said, "well, I bet the hotel was just like I described."

"No, quite the opposite! They'd just finished a $25 million remodeling. It's the finest hotel in Rome, now. They were overbooked, so they apologized and gave us the Presidential suite for no extra charge!"

"Well," Joe mumbled, "I know you didn't get to see the Pope!"

"Actually, we were quite lucky. As we toured the Vatican, a Swiss guard tapped me on the shoulder and explained the Pope likes to personally meet some of the visitors, and if I'd be so kind as to step into this private room and wait, the Pope would personally greet me. Sure enough, after 5 minutes the Pope walked through the door and shook my hand. I knelt down as he spoke a few words to me."

Impressed, Joe asked, "Tell me, please! What'd he say?"

"Oh, not much really. Just 'Where'd you get that awful haircut?'"

*   *   *

John: "I just fell off a 30-foot ladder."

Bob: "Are you OK?"

John: "Yeah, luckily I was just on the first step."

*   *   *

A game warden noticed how a particular fellow named Sam consistently caught more fish than anyone else. Whereas the other guys would only catch three or four a day, Sam would come in off the lake with a boat full. Stringer after stringer was always packed with freshly caught trout. The warden, curious, asked Sam his secret. The successful fisherman invited the game warden to accompany him and observe.

So the next morning the two met at the dock and took off in Sam's boat. When they got to the middle of the lake, Sam stopped the boat, and the warden sat back to see how it was done.

Sam's approach was simple. He took out a stick of dynamite, lit it, and threw it in the air. The explosion rocked the lake with such a force that dead fish immediately began to surface. Sam took out a net and started scooping them up.

When the game warden recovered from the shock, he began yelling at Sam. "You can't do this! I'll put you in jail, buddy! You'll be paying every fine in the book!"

Sam set his net down and took out another stick of dynamite. He lit it and tossed it in the lap of the game warden with these words, "Are you going to sit there all day complaining, or are you going to fish?"

* * *

Sherlock Holmes and Dr. Watson went on a camping trip. After a good meal and a bottle of wine, they lay down for the night and went to sleep.

Some hours later, Holmes awoke and nudged his faithful friend. "Watson, look up and tell me what you see."

Watson replied, "I see millions and millions of stars."

"What does that tell you?"

Watson pondered for a minute. "Astronomically, it tells me that there are millions of galaxies and planets. Astrologically, I observe that Saturn is in Leo. Horologically, I deduce that the time is approximately a quarter past three. Theologically, I can see that God is all powerful and that we are small and insignificant. Meteorologically, I suspect that we will have a beautiful day tomorrow. Why, what does it tell YOU?"

Holmes said, "Watson, you idiot. Some jerk has stolen our tent."

* * *

A cannibal went to the tribe's witch doctor. "Doc, I've been feeling lousy lately."

"Hmmm," replied the witch doctor. "Let's review your diet. Are you eating man or animal?"

"Man, doc. We're eating those Catholic missionaries we caught last week."

"OK, tell me how you cook them."

"Same way as always, doc. We boil them up in the big pot."

"Hmmm," pondered the witch doctor. "Tell me more about these Catholic missionaries."

"Well, funny thing, doc. They all look alike! They're short, fat, wear long robes, sandals, rope for belts, and are bald with a fringe of hair."

"Well, that's your problem right there," said the witch doctor. "Those guys aren't boilers! They're friars!"

* * *

One day two carrots were walking down the street. They were the best of friends. Just as they started to step off the curb a car came speeding around the corner and ran one of them over. The unhurt carrot cradled his buddy, telling him over and over again that he would be OK. Finally the ambulance arrived and rushed the injured carrot off to the hospital. His friend rode with him. Once at the hospital the uninjured carrot paced back and forth in the emergency room waiting to hear how his pal was going to be.

After many minutes of agonized waiting the doctor came out. He walked over to the distraught carrot and said, "I have good news and I have bad news. The good news is that your friend is going to be all right. The bad news is that he is going to be a vegetable for the rest of his life."

* * *

From a passenger ship, everyone could see a bearded man on a small island, who was shouting and desperately waving his hands.

"Who is that man and why is he so upset?" a passenger asked the captain.

"I've no idea, but every year when we pass by, he goes nuts."

* * *

Tech support: "Okay Bob, let's press the control and escape keys at the same time. That brings up a task list in the middle of the screen. Now type the letter P to bring up the Program Manager."

Customer: "I don't have a P."

Tech support: "On your keyboard, Bob."

Customer: "What do you mean?"

Tech support: "P . . . on your keyboard, Bob."

Customer: "I'M NOT GOING TO DO THAT!!"

* * *

"Oh, no!" he gasped as he surveyed the disaster before him. Never in his 40 years of life had he seen anything like it. How anyone could have survived he did not know.

He could only hope that somewhere amid the overwhelming destruction he would find his 16-year-old son. Only the slim hope of finding Danny kept him from turning and fleeing the scene. He took a deep breath and proceeded.

Walking was virtually impossible with so many things strewn across his path. He moved ahead slowly.

"Danny! Danny!" he whispered to himself. He tripped and almost fell several times. He heard someone, or something, move. At least he thought he did. Perhaps he was just hoping he did. He shook his head and felt his gut tighten.

He couldn't understand how this could have happened. There was some light but not enough to see very much. Something cold and wet brushed against his hand. He jerked it away.

In desperation, he took another step, then cried out, "Danny!"

From a nearby pile of unidentified material, he heard his son. "Yes, Dad," he said, in a voice so weak it could hardly be heard.

"It's time to get up and get ready for school," the man sighed, "and, good grief, clean up this room!"

* * *

Phil goes to Europe and leaves his favorite dog with his brother James. While in Europe, Phil calls James to check on his dog and asks, "So James, how's my favorite dog doing?"

James very tersely replies, "Your dog is dead."

"What?" says Phil. "You can't just tell someone their favorite dog is dead without a warning; you have to ease them into it."

"How?" asks James.

"Well, the first day I call, tell me my dog is on the roof. Then tell me the dog is going to be fine and not to worry. The next day, when I call to ask about my dog, tell me that you were about to get it down, when it jumped off of the roof and broke its leg. Tell me the doctors say it will be OK, but that it will have to stay at the vet's for a while. Are you getting all of this?"

"Yes," says James.

"Good," says Phil. "Then the next day when I call back, tell me that there was severe internal bleeding that the vet didn't pick up and that my favorite dog died at 2:00 this morning. That way it won't be such a shock to me. Got it?"

"Yes."

"Good, so, how's Grandma doing?" asks Phil.

"Well," James replies, "she's on the roof."

* * *

A man had been drinking at a pub all night. The bartender finally said that the bar was closing. So the man stood up to leave and fell flat on his face. He tried to stand one more time; same result. He figured he'd crawl outside and get some fresh air and maybe that would sober him up.

Once outside he stood up and fell flat on his face. So he decided to crawl the four blocks to his home. When he arrived at the door he stood up and again fell flat on his face. He crawled through the door and into his bedroom. When he reached his bed he tried one more time to stand up. This time he managed to pull himself upright, but he quickly fell right into bed and was sound asleep as soon as his head hit the pillow.

He was awakened the next morning to his wife standing over him, shouting, "So, you've been out drinking again!!"

"What makes you say that?" he asked, putting on an innocent look.

"The pub called. You left your wheelchair there again."

* * *

A knight and his men returned to their castle after a long hard day of fighting.

"How are we faring?" asked the king.

"Sire," replied the knight, "I have been robbing and pillaging on your behalf all day, burning the towns of your enemies in the west."

"What?!?" shrieked the king. "I don't have any enemies in the west!"

"Oh," said the knight. "Well, you do now."

* * *

A farm boy accidentally overturned his wagonload of wheat on the road. The farmer that lived nearby came to investigate. "Hey, Willis," he called out, "forget your troubles for a while and come and have dinner with us. Then I'll help you turn the wagon back over."

"That's very nice of you," Willis answered, "but I don't think Dad would like me to."

"Aw, come on, son!" the farmer insisted.

"Well, OK," the boy finally agreed, "but Dad won't like it."

After a hearty dinner, Willis thanked the host. "I feel a lot better now, but I know Dad's going to be real upset."

"Don't be silly!" said the neighbor. "By the way, where is he?"

"Under the wagon," replied Willis.

* * *

Once there was a golfer whose drive landed on an anthill. Rather than move the ball, he decided to hit it where it lay. He gave a mighty swing. Clouds of dirt and sand and ants exploded from the spot. Everything but the golf ball. It sat in the same spot.

So he lined up and tried another shot. Clouds of dirt and sand and ants went flying again. The golf ball didn't even wiggle.

Two ants survived. One dazed ant said to the other, "What are we going to do?"

Said the other ant, "If we're going to save ourselves, we'd better get on the ball."

* * *

One lovely morning, Ben and Thomas were out golfing. Ben sliced his ball deep into a wooded ravine. He grabbed his 8-iron and proceeded down the embankment into the ravine in search of his ball. He searched diligently through the thick underbrush and suddenly he spotted something shiny. As he got closer, he realized that the shiny object was in fact an 8-iron in the hands of a skeleton lying near an old golf ball.

Ben excitedly called out to his golfing partner, "Hey Thomas, come here, I got big trouble down here."

Thomas came running over to the edge of the ravine and called out, "What's the matter, Ben?"

Ben yelled back in a nervous voice, "Throw me my 7-iron! Looks like you can't get out of here with an 8-iron."

* * *

A plane was taking off from Kennedy Airport. After it reached a comfortable cruising altitude, the captain announced over the intercom, "Ladies and gentlemen, this is your captain speaking. Welcome to Flight 293, nonstop from New York to Los Angeles. The weather ahead is good and we should have a smooth and uneventful flight. Now sit back and relax—OH MY GOSH!" Silence.

Then, the captain came back on the intercom and said, "Ladies and Gentlemen, I am so sorry if I scared you earlier, but while I was talking, the flight attendant brought me a cup of hot coffee and spilled it in my lap. You should see the front of my pants!"

A passenger in Coach said, "That's nothing. He should see the back of mine!"

* * *

A young man volunteered for Navy service during World War II. He had such a high aptitude for aviation that he was sent right to Pensacola, skipping boot camp. The very first day, he soloed and was the best flier on the base. All they could do was give him his gold wings and assign him immediately to an aircraft carrier in the Pacific.

On his first day aboard, he took off and single-handedly shot down six Japanese zeroes. Then climbing up to 20,000 ft., he found nine more Japanese planes and shot them all down, too. Noting that his fuel was getting low, he descended, circled the carrier, and came in for a perfect landing on the deck.

He threw back the canopy, climbed out, and jogged over to the captain. Saluting smartly, he said, "Well, sir, how did I do on my very first day?"

The captain turned around, bowed, and replied, "You make one velly impoltant mistake!"

* * *

A musical chord walks into a bar wanting a drink. The bartender looks at the chord and says, "I'm sorry. I can't serve you. You're A minor."

* * *

A young couple were touring southern Florida and happened to stop at a rattlesnake farm along the road. After seeing the sights, they engaged in small talk with the man that handled the snakes.

"Gosh!" exclaimed the new bride. "You certainly have a dangerous job. Do you ever get bitten by the snakes?"

"Yes, on rare occasions," answered the handler.

"Well," she continued, "just what do you do when you're bitten by a snake?"

"I always carry a razor-sharp knife in my pocket, and as soon as I am bitten, I make deep criss-cross marks across the fang entry and then suck the poison from the wound."

"What, uh . . . what would happen if you accidentally sat on a rattler?" persisted the woman.

"Ma'am," answered the snake handler, "that will be the day I learn who my real friends are."

* * *

Two Spanish detectives were investigating the murder of Juan Gonzalez.

"How was he killed?" asked one detective.

"With a golf gun," the other detective replied.

"A golf gun! What is a golf gun?"

"I don't know. But it sure made a hole in Juan."

*   *   *

A man in Alabama had a flat tire, pulled off on the side of the road, and proceeded to put a bouquet of flowers in front of the car and one behind it. Then he got back in the car to wait.

A passerby studied the scene as he drove by, and was so curious he turned around and went back. He asked the fellow what the problem was. The man replied, "I got a flat tahr."

The passerby asked, "But what's with the flowers?"

The man said, "When you break down, they tell you to put flares in the front and flares in the back."

*   *   *

A man lay spread out over three seats in the second row of a movie theatre. As he lay there breathing heavily, an usher came over and said, "That's very rude of you, sir, taking up three seats. Didn't you learn any manners? Where did you come from?"

The man looked up helplessly and said, "The balcony!"

*   *   *

A woman goes to the doctor for her yearly physical. The nurse starts with certain basic items. "How much do you weigh?" she asks.

"120," the woman says. The nurse puts her on the scale. It turns out her weight is 150.

The nurse asks, "Your height?"

"5 feet, 8 inches," she says. The nurse checks and sees that she measures only 5 feet, 5 inches.

She then takes her blood pressure and tells the woman it is very high.

"Of course it's high!" she screams. "When I came in here, I was tall and slender, and now I'm short and fat!"

* * *

A fellow went to the doctor, who told him that he had a bad illness and only a year to live. So he decided to talk to his pastor, and, after he explained his situation, asked if there was anything he could do.

"What you should do is go out and buy a late 70's or early 80's model Dodge pickup," said the pastor. "Then go get married to the meanest woman you can find, and buy yourselves an old trailer house in the panhandle of Oklahoma."

The fellow asked, "Will this help me live longer?"

"No," said the pastor, "but it will make what time you do have seem like forever."

* * *

A certain little girl, when asked her name, would reply, "I'm Mr. Browning's daughter."

Her mother told her this was wrong. She must say, "I'm Jane Browning."

The minister spoke to her in Sunday School, and said, "Aren't you Mr. Browning's daughter?"

She replied, "I thought I was, but mother says I'm not."

* * *

Recorded telephone message: "Hi. I'm probably home. I'm just avoiding someone I don't like. Leave me a message, and if I don't call back, it's you."

* * *

The Smiths were proud of their family tradition. Their ancestors had come to America on the Mayflower. They had included Senators and Wall Street wizards.

They decided to compile a family history, a legacy for their children and grandchildren. They hired a fine author. Only one problem arose—how to handle that great-uncle George, who was executed in the electric chair. The author said he could handle the story tactfully.

The book appeared. It said, "Great-uncle George occupied a chair of applied electronics at an important government institution, was attached to his position by the strongest of ties, and his death came as a great shock."

*   *   *

"You know, it's at times like these when I'm trapped in an airlock with an alien and about to die of asphyxiation in deep space that I really wish I'd listened to what my mother told me when I was young!"

"Why, what did she tell you?"

"I don't know, I didn't listen!"

*   *   *

For weeks, a 6-year-old boy kept telling his first-grade teacher about the baby brother or sister that was expected at his house. One day his mother allowed the boy to feel the movements of the unborn child. The 6-year-old was obviously impressed, but he made no comment. Furthermore, he stopped telling his teacher about the impending event.

The teacher finally sat the boy on her lap and said, "Tommy, whatever became of that baby brother or sister you were expecting at home?"

Tommy burst into tears and confessed, "I think Mommy ate it!"

*   *   *

A couple lived near the ocean and used to walk the beach a lot. One summer they noticed a girl who was at the beach pretty much every day. She wasn't unusual, nor was the travel bag she carried, except for one thing. She would approach people who were sitting on the beach, glance around furtively, then speak to them.

Generally, the people would respond negatively and she would wander off, but occasionally someone would nod and there would be a quick exchange of money for something she carried in her bag. The couple assumed she was selling drugs and debated calling the cops, but since they didn't know for sure they just continued to watch her.

After a couple of weeks the wife asked, "Honey, have you ever noticed that she only goes up to people with boom boxes and other electronic devices?" He said he hadn't. Then she said, "Tomorrow I want you to get a towel and our big radio and go lie out on the beach. Then we can find out what she's really doing."

Well, the plan went off without a hitch, and the wife was almost hopping up and down with anticipation when she saw the girl talk to her husband and then leave. The man walked up the beach and met his wife at the road. "Well, is she selling drugs?" she asked excitedly.

"No, she's not," he said.

"Well, what is it, then?" his wife fairly shrieked.

The man grinned and said, "She's a battery salesperson."

"Batteries?" cried the wife.

"Yes" he replied. "She sells C cells by the seashore."

* * *

Two friends, one an Optimist and the other a Pessimist, could never quite agree on any topic of discussion. One day the Optimist decided he had found a good way to pull his friend out of his continual Pessimistic thinking.

The Optimist owned a hunting dog that could walk on water. He decided to take the Pessimist and the dog out duck hunting in a boat. They got out into the middle of the lake, and the Optimist brought down a duck. The dog immediately walked out across the water, retrieved the duck, and walked back to the boat.

The Optimist looked at his Pessimistic friend and said, "What do you think about that?"

The Pessimist replied, "That dog can't swim, can he?"

* * *

A guy goes to a girl's house for the first time and she shows him into the living room. She excuses herself to go to the kitchen to get them a drink. As he's standing there alone, he notices a cute little vase on the mantel. He picks it up and as he's looking at it, she walks back in. He says, "What's this?"

She says, "Oh, my father's ashes are in there."

He turns beat red in horror and goes, "Oh . . . I . . ."

She says, "Yeah, he's too lazy to go to the kitchen to get an ashtray."

*   *   *

A redneck came home and found his house on fire, rushed next door, telephoned the fire department and shouted, "Hurry on over here. My house is on fire!"

"OK," replied the fireman, "how do we get there?"

"Don't you still have them big red trucks?"

*   *   *

A guy was at a hotel, and took his computer down to the bar to do some data entries. He asked the bartender, "What's the wifi password?"

Bartender: "You need to buy a drink first."

Guy: "Okay, I'll have a cola."

Bartender: "We have Coke, no Pepsi."

Guy: "Sure. How much is it?"

Bartender: "$3.00."

Guy: "OK. Here you are. What's the wifi password?"

Bartender: "youneedtobuyadrinkfirst, no spaces and all lowercase . . ."

*   *   *

The coed came running in tears to her father. "Dad, you gave me some terrible financial advice!" she cried.

"I did? What did I tell you?" asked the dad.

"You told me to put my money in that big bank, and now that big bank is in trouble."

"What are you talking about? That's one of the largest banks in the world," he said. "Surely there must be some mistake."

"I don't think so," she sniffed. "They just returned one of my checks with a note saying, 'Insufficient Funds.'"

* * *

The Cleveland Symphony was performing Beethoven's Ninth. In the piece, there's a long passage, about 20 minutes, during which the bass violinists have nothing to do. Rather than sit around that whole time looking stupid, some bassists decided to sneak offstage and go to the tavern next door for a quick beer. After gulping several beers in quick succession, one of them looked at his watch. "Hey! We need to get back!"

"No need to panic," said a fellow bassist. "I thought we might need some extra time, so I tied the last few pages of the conductor's score together with string. It'll take him a few minutes to get it untangled." A few moments later, they staggered back to the concert hall and took their places in the orchestra.

About this time, a member of the audience noticed the conductor seemed a bit edgy and said as much to her companion. "Well, of course," said her companion. "Don't you see? It's the bottom of the Ninth, the score is tied, and the basses are loaded."

* * *

A hungry traveler ordered some "old-fashioned bean and ox-tail soup" at a roadside diner. After waiting ten minutes he was so hungry he felt he couldn't bear it another minute. Across the table a customer with a nearly full bowl of the soup was reading a newspaper while it cooled. Carefully he reached over and pulled the soup to his side of the table. It smelled so good he grabbed his spoon and gulped it down, thinking that he'd give his fresh bowl of soup to the man when it arrived. The soup was delicious! But he apparently ate it too fast, because no sooner had he finished the bowl than his stomach reacted and he vomited every bit of it right back into the bowl. The man across the way lowered his newspaper and said, "I know how you feel. The same thing happened to me just a little while ago."

*   *   *

A sign on a dryer in the laundromat said, "This dryer is worthless." A sign on the next dryer said, "This dryer is next to worthless."

*   *   *

Three numbskulls were in the forest when they spotted a set of tracks.

The first one said, "Hey, deer tracks!"

The second one said, "No, dog tracks!"

The third one said, "You're both crazy—they're cow tracks!"

They were still arguing when the train hit them.

*   *   *

A dim-witted king was losing a territorial dispute with a neighboring monarch. As the fight wore on, he got more and more frustrated until finally he roared, "Where are my two court jesters?"

In seconds two jesters appeared at his side. "Okay, let's continue," he said, "now that I have my wits about me."

*   *   *

Some New Yorkers were on a safari in the jungles of a faraway country when they were captured by cannibals. The chief of the tribe gloated, "We're going to put you all into big pots of water, cook you, and eat you."

"You can't do that to me," the tour leader said. "I'm the editor of *The New Yorker*!"

"Well," he replied, "tonight you will be editor-in-chief!"

*   *   *

A Russian cosmonaut had an emergency during his reentry into earth's atmosphere, and his spacecraft crash landed in the Australian bush, in the middle of nowhere. After what seemed an eternity, he woke up in a bush hospital clinic, very rustic and dirty, with foul smells, and he was bandaged from head to foot. He saw a very large, gruff-looking nurse approaching him as he lay in his cot.

"Did I come here to die?" he said with a deep sense of resignation and fear.

"No," the Aussie nurse replied. "You came here yesterday."

* * *

Three men were canoeing down the Amazon River when they were captured by cannibals. They were told they would each get one last wish before they were skinned and made into boats.

The first man wished for a last meal. He was given a sumptuous meal, which was specially prepared with all the best ingredients.

The second man wished to be married to the most beautiful woman in the tribe. His wish was granted for his last remaining day.

The third man wished simply for a fork. The confused village elders gave him a fork, then watched in horror as he poked himself full of holes and said, "Ain't nobody making a boat out of me!"

* * *

A young man walked into an insurance office to get coverage for his new motorcycle. One question confused him: "Do you have a lien holder on the vehicle?"

"I've got a kickstand," he replied. "Is that the same thing?"

* * *

A man saw a letter lying on his doormat. It said on the envelope, "DO NOT BEND." He spent the next two hours trying to figure out how to pick it up.

* * *

A man called his mother in Florida. "Mom, how are you?" he asked.

"Not too good," she said. "I've been very weak."

The son said, "Why are you so weak?"

She said, "Because I haven't eaten in 36 days."

The son said, "That's terrible. Why haven't you eaten in 36 days?"

The mother answered, "I didn't want my mouth to be filled with food if you should call."

＊　＊　＊

"Listen, Captain," said a police officer, "we've been giving that ventriloquist the third degree for over an hour and a half, and a plainclothesman, three cops, and a detective have all confessed to the crime. Should we keep going?"

＊　＊　＊

"I'm not going to wear those pants any longer."

"Why not?"

"They're long enough now."

＊　＊　＊

A potential customer was wandering the aisles of a specialty food shop. "We're having a sale on tongue," a clerk said. "Would you like some?"

"Ugh!" growled the woman. "I would never eat anything from an animal's mouth!"

"In that case, how about a dozen eggs?"

＊　＊　＊

"I hope you paid your taxes with a smile last month."

"I wanted to, but the man insisted on cash."

＊　＊　＊

A woman was in a car wreck and suffered a cut on her head. She went to a doctor who shaved off some of her hair and sewed up the cut. She was a little perturbed about the stitches and asked, "Will there be any scars in my crown?"

＊　＊　＊

On a hot summer day, a man decided to lay a cement sidewalk from his porch out to the street. He worked all day on it, and finally finished it in mid-afternoon. As he was putting his tools away, and the cement was half dry, his wife came out on the porch and said, "Honey, you've done a great job. I just made a pitcher of iced tea. Why don't you come inside and we'll sit in the living room together and have some nice cold sweet tea?"

That sounded wonderful to her husband, so they went in together and they cooled off and drank her excellent tea and talked. A few minutes later, the man heard a voice in the front yard and went to the curtains and looked outside. What he saw made him dash to the door, run out on the porch, and scream at a neighborhood kid who was tromping through his cement, leaving gigantic holes in his carefully leveled sidewalk, "Hey you, get off my sidewalk! What do you think you're doing?" His neck was red and he looked ready to jump down and take a swing at the kid.

His wife followed him onto the porch and put her arm around him. "Honey," she said, "relax. You know you love children."

Her husband replied, "Yes, I do. I love children in the abstract, but not in the concrete!"

*   *   *

There was this little guy sitting in a bar, drinking away, minding his own business, when all of a sudden this great big dude came in and WHACK!! knocked him off the bar stool and onto the floor. The big dude said, "That was a karate chop from Korea."

The little guy thought, "Weird," but he got back up on the stool and started drinking again, when all of a sudden WHACK!! the big dude knocked him down AGAIN and said, "That was a judo chop from Japan."

The little guy had had enough of this. He got up, brushed himself off and quietly left.

The little guy was gone for an hour or so when he returned. Without saying a word, he walked up behind the big dude and WHAM!!! knocked the big dude off his stool, knocking him out cold!!!

The little guy looked at the bartender and said, "When he comes to, tell him that's a crowbar from Sears."

*   *   *

An astronomer is on an expedition to Borneo to observe a total eclipse of the sun, which will only be observable there, when he's captured by cannibals.

The eclipse is due the next day around noon. To gain his freedom he plans to pose as a god and threaten to extinguish the sun if he's not released, but the timing has to be just right. So, in the few words of the cannibals' language that he knows, he asks his guard what time they plan to kill him.

The guard answers, "Tradition has it that captives are to be killed when the sun reaches the highest point in the sky on the day after their capture so that they may be cooked and ready to be served for the evening meal."

"Great," the astronomer replies.

The guard continues, though, "But because everyone's so excited about it, in your case we're going to wait until after the eclipse."

*   *   *

They say you are what you eat. Lay off the nuts.

*   *   *

Literary Insults:

"I have never killed a man, but I have read many obituaries with great pleasure." - Clarence Darrow

"There's nothing wrong with you that reincarnation won't cure." - Jack E. Leonard

"He can compress the most words into the smallest idea of any man I know." - Abraham Lincoln

"I've had a perfectly wonderful evening. But this wasn't it." - Groucho Marx

"I didn't attend the funeral, but I sent a nice letter saying I approved of it." - Mark Twain

"He has no enemies, but is intensely disliked by his friends." - Oscar Wilde

"He has Van Gogh's ear for music." - Billy Wilder

School Daze

A teacher was giving a lesson on the circulation of the blood. Trying to make the matter clearer, he said, "Now, boys, if I stood on my head, the blood, as you know, would run into it, and I would turn red in the face."

"Yes, sir," the boys said.

"Then why is it that while I am standing upright in the ordinary position, the blood doesn't run into my feet?"

A little fellow shouted, "Cause yer feet ain't empty."

* * *

A second grader came home from school and said to her grandmother, "Grandma, guess what? We learned how to make babies today."

The grandmother, surprised, tried to keep her cool. "That's interesting. How do you make babies?"

"It's simple," replied the girl. "You just change 'y' to 'i' and add 'es.'"

* * *

A college professor asked his class a question.

"If Philadelphia is 100 miles from New York and Chicago is 1,000 miles from Philadelphia and Los Angeles is 2,000 miles from Chicago, how old am I?"

One student in the back of the class raised his hand and said, "Professor, you're 44."

The professor said, "You're absolutely correct, but tell me, how did you arrive at the answer so quickly?"

The student said, "You see, professor, I have a brother; he's 22, and he's only half crazy."

* * *

A statistics major was completely out of it the day of his final exam. It was a true/false test, so he decided to flip a coin for the answers. The stats professor watched the student the entire two hours as he was flipping the coin . . . writing the answer . . . flipping the coin . . . writing the answer.

At the end of the two hours, everyone else had left the final except for the one student. The professor walked up to the student's desk and interrupted him, saying, "Listen, I have seen that you did not study for this statistics test, and you didn't even open the exam. If you are just flipping a coin for your answers, what's taking you so long?"

The student replied bitterly, as he was still flipping the coin, "I'm checking my answers!"

*   *   *

A Mississippi student was visiting a relative in Boston over the holidays. He went to a large party and met a pretty coed. He attempted to start up a conversation using the line, "Where do y'all go to school?"

The coed was not impressed with his grammar or southern drawl but did answer his question. "Yale," she replied.

The other student took a big deep breath and shouted, "WHERE DO Y'ALL GO TO SCHOOL?"

*   *   *

My mom said she learned how to swim when someone took her out in the lake and threw her off the boat.

I said, "Mom, they weren't trying to teach you how to swim."

*   *   *

I'm reading a book on the history of glue.

I can't put it down.

*   *   *

An English professor was reading Canterbury Tales to his class and noticed that one of his students had fallen asleep. The professor was annoyed enough to send the book spinning through the air and bounce it off the sleeper's skull. Startled awake, the student asked what had hit him.

"That," said the professor, "was a flying Chaucer."

* * *

A child came home from his first day at school.

His mother asked, "Well, what did you learn today?"

The kid replied, "Not enough. They want me to come back tomorrow."

* * *

"Teacher," said the eight-year-old, "I don't want to scare you, but my daddy says that if I don't get better grades, someone is going to get spanked."

* * *

The cross-eyed teacher had trouble controlling his pupils.

* * *

Leaping Spark was one of the brightest boys in his Indian tribe and his progress was watched closely by the chief. When he had completed his grades in the reservation school, the chief decided he should be sent to university.

Leaping Spark didn't let the tribe down. He graduated magna cum laude as an electrical engineer. In gratitude, he decided he would decorate the entrance to the reservation's longhouse with a moose head that would glow in the dark.

He installed lights for the eyes and twined other lights around the antlers. In the evening it was a landmark to be seen for miles!

And so Leaping Spark became the first Native American ever to wire a head for a reservation.

* * *

The fourth-grade teacher had to leave the room for a few minutes. When she returned, she found the children in perfect order.

Everybody was sitting absolutely quiet. She was shocked and stunned, and said, "I've never seen anything like it before. This is wonderful. But, please tell me, what came over all of you? Why are you so well behaved and quiet?"

Finally, after much urging, little Sally spoke up and said, "Well, one time you said that if you ever came back and found us quiet, you would drop dead."

* * *

In my teaching job I had a kid who threatened to kill me one year because I gave him an F. Another teacher caught him writing "Kill Dr. B." in his weekly planner in the section labeled "Weekly Goals and Objectives." The school was freaking out. They didn't know what to do about it. They kept asking me if I felt threatened, and I was like, "Why? This kid hasn't met any of his goals all year."

* * *

The teacher gave her fifth grade class an assignment: get their parents to tell them a story with a moral at the end of it. The next day the kids came back and one by one began to tell their stories.

Kathy said, "My father's a farmer and we have a lot of hens. One time we were taking our eggs to the market in a basket on the front seat of the pickup when we hit a bump in the road all the eggs went flying and broke and made a mess."

"And what's the moral of the story?" asked the teacher.

"Don't put all your eggs in one basket!"

"Very good," said the teacher. "Now, Lucy?"

"Our family are farmers too. But we raise chickens for the meat market. We had a dozen eggs one time but when they hatched we only got ten live chicks. And the moral to this story is, Don't count your chickens until they're hatched."

"That was a fine story, Lucy. Johnny, do you have a story to share?"

"Yes, ma'am, my daddy told me this story about my uncle Bob. Uncle Bob was a pilot in Vietnam and his plane got hit. He had to bail out over enemy territory and all he had was a bottle of whiskey, a machine gun, and a machete. He drank the whiskey on the way down so it wouldn't break and then he landed right in the middle of 100 enemy troops. He killed seventy of them with the machine gun until he ran out of bullets, then he killed twenty more with the machete till the blade broke and then he killed the last ten with his bare hands."

"Good heavens," said the horrified teacher, "what kind of moral did your daddy tell you from that horrible story?"

"Don't mess with Uncle Bob when he's been drinking."

* * *

An English professor announced to the class, "There are two words I don't allow in my class. One is gross and the other is cool."

From the back of the room a voice called out, "So, what are the words?"

* * *

Children were called upon in class to make sentences with words chosen by the teacher. The teacher smiled when Jack, a slow learner, raised his hand to participate during the challenge with the words "Defeat," "Defense," "Deduct," and "Detail." Jack stood and all eyes focused on him as his classmates awaited his reply. Smiling, he proudly shouted out, "Defeat of deduct went over defense before detail."

* * *

The teacher asked, "Johnny, what is the chemical formula for water?"

Johnny replied, "H I J K L M N O."

The teacher exclaimed, "What are you talking about?"

Johnny said, "Yesterday you said it's H to O."

* * *

A Texas kid and his mom were walking down a sidewalk in Lubbock. The kid saw some cowboys and said, "Hey Maw, look at them thar men with them thar bowed laigs."

His mom said that if he didn't start speaking correct English, she was going to send him to a Shakespearean English school.

A little farther along, they saw some more cowboys. "Hey maw! Look at them thar men with them thar bowed laigs!" he said.

True to her word, she sent him off to a Shakespearean English school to learn correct English. He came home several months later on vacation. As they walked together down the sidewalk, they saw some cowboys. "Hark!" he said. "What manner of men are these who wear their legs in parentheses?"

* * *

Did you hear about the kidnapping at school?

It's OK. He woke up.

* * *

A reporter said to a college basketball coach, "Your player is great on the court, but how is his academic work?"

"He makes straight A's," said the coach.

"Excellent!" said the reporter, making notes.

"Right," said the coach, "but his B's are a little crooked."

* * *

Two highway workers were at a construction site when a car with diplomatic plates pulled up.

"*Parlez-vous français*?" the driver asked. The two just stared.

"*Hablan ustedes español*?" the driver tried next. They stared some more.

"*Sprechen Sie Deutsch*?" They continued to stare.

"*Parlate italiano*?" They said nothing. Finally the man drove off in disgust.

One worker turned to the other and said, "Maybe we should learn a foreign language."

"What for?" the other one replied. "That guy knew four of them, and a fat lot of good it did him."

* * *

A prison inmate kept missing his required classes. First it was because he had a tooth pulled. Then his tonsils were taken out. Next he chopped off the tip of his finger in a workshop. A guard commented, "We'd better keep an eye on this guy. He seems to be trying to escape one piece at a time."

* * *

"I've just had the most awful time," said a boy to his friends. "First I got angina pectoris, then arteriosclerosis. Just as I was recovering, I got psoriasis. They gave me hypodermics, and to top it all, tonsillitis was followed by appendectomy."

"Wow! How did you pull through?" his friends asked.

"I don't know," the boy replied. "Toughest spelling test I ever had."

* * *

Teacher: "Tommy, why are you scratching yourself?"

Tommy: "No one else knows where I itch."

* * *

"Let's hope you did well in the ratings," the TV star told his son when the boy handed him his report card.

"I sure did, Dad," was the reply. "They want to sign me up to do another 13 weeks this summer."

* * *

The professor was testing his class in logic and said, "Last year people bought ten million quarter-inch drills. Why?"

After a brief stillness, one bright student answered, "Obviously, they wanted quarter-inch drills."

"No, not at all," the professor replied. "They wanted quarter-inch holes."

* * *

Sometimes my childhood friends would skip school and then write their own excuse notes: "Mary could not come to school because she has been bothered by very close veins." "Please excuse Tom for being absent yesterday. He had diarrhea and his boots leak." "Please excuse my son's tardiness. I forgot to wake him up and I did not find him till I started making the beds." "Please excuse Harriet for missing school yesterday. We forgot to get the Sunday paper off the porch, and when we found it Monday, we thought it was Sunday."

* * *

The heaviest element known to science was recently discovered by chemists. The element, tentatively named Administratum, has no protons or electrons and thus has an atomic number of zero.

However it does have:

1 neutron.

125 assistant neutrons

75 vice-neutrons

111 assistant vice-neutrons

This gives it an atomic mass of 312. The 312 particles are held together by a force that involves the continuous exchange of meson-like particles called morons.

Since it has no electrons, Administratum is inert. However, it can be detected chemically as it impedes every action with which it comes in contact. According to the discoverers, a minute amount of Administratum causes one reaction to take four days to complete when it would have normally occurred in less than one second.

Administratum has a normal half-life of approximately three years, at which time it does not actually decay but instead undergoes a reorganization in which assistant neutrons, vice-neutrons, and assistant vice-neutrons exchange places. Some studies have shown that atomic mass actually increases after each reorganization.

Research at other laboratories indicates that Administratum occurs naturally in the atmosphere. It tends to concentrate at certain points such as government agencies, large corporations, and universities and can usually be found in the newest, best appointed, and best maintained buildings.

Chemists point out that Administratum is known to be toxic at any level of concentration and can easily destroy any productive reaction where it is allowed to accumulate. Attempts are being made to determine how Administratum can be controlled to prevent irreversible damage, but results to date are not promising.

Far Out, Dude!

As I was eating breakfast, I started thinking about all the problems I faced in my life. Suddenly I grabbed a knife and my box of raisin bran, and began stabbing it, again and again, until it lay in shreds on the table before me. And then I realized what I had become: a cereal killer.

*   *   *

John and Bob went fishing one summer and decided to rent a boat from the resort instead of fishing from the shore. They rowed out a little way and started to fish. They caught one fish after another.

John said to Bob, "I wish we could mark this spot. It's the best fishing I've seen since I was a boy."

Bob replied, "I got some chalk in my tackle box, so why don't I put an X right here on the bottom of the boat?"

John laughed, "You goofball! What if we don't rent the same boat next time?"

*   *   *

A farm boy visited a big city for the first time. He was really amazed by all the buildings and offices downtown, and even the weird little shops, like one with signs that read: "Palm-reading," "Fortunes told here," "Ancestors contacted here." So he went inside and saw a table covered with a green cloth and a glass ball in the center. There was a chair on each side, and behind it a sign read, "Sit down and wait." So he sat and waited. And waited, and waited, and waited.

After about 20 minutes, he was about to get up and leave when suddenly a woman in a long robe with a turban on her head entered the room through a curtain and sat down opposite him. She didn't say anything, but began to rub the glass ball. As she rubbed it, she began to chuckle a little; then she giggled and finally began to laugh. Suddenly the farm boy stood up, grabbed the woman by her neck, and slugged her right in the jaw, leaving her unconscious on the floor.

When he got home and told his friends about his day in the big city, they asked him, "Why did you slug that lady?"

He answered, "Well, it's something my daddy used to tell me. He said, 'Son, always strike a happy medium.' So I did!"

*   *   *

My cousin married an invisible woman. The kids are nothing to look at either.

*   *   *

A young guy came running into the country store and said to his buddy, "Bubba, somebody just stole your pickup truck from the parking lot!"

Bubba replied, "Did you see who it was?"

The young man answered, "No, but I got the license number."

*   *   *

An Alabama state trooper pulled over a pickup. The trooper asked, "Got any ID?"

The driver replied, "Bout whut?"

*   *   *

An elderly woman lived on a small farm in Canada, just yards away from the North Dakota border. Their land had been the subject of a minor dispute between the United States and Canada for years. The now widowed woman lived on the farm with her son and three grandchildren. One day her son came into her room holding a letter.

"I just got some news, Mom," he said. "The government has come to an agreement with the people in North Dakota. They've decided that our land is really part of the United States. We have the right to approve or disapprove of the agreement. What do you think?"

"What do I think?" his mother said. "Sign it! Call them right now and tell them we accept! I don't think I could stand another one of those Canadian winters!"

*   *   *

I went to the Air and Space Museum, but there was nothing there.

*   *   *

They're not going to make yardsticks any longer.

* * *

At a preliminary training session for parachute jumping, the instructor talked about preparing for landing when you reach 300 feet.

A woman asked, "How do you know when you're at 300 feet?"

"A good question," replied the instructor. "At 300 feet you can recognize the faces of people on the ground."

The woman thought about this for a moment and said, "What happens if there's no one there I know?"

* * *

A man went into a restaurant and was enjoying a drink and some nuts before his meal came, when suddenly he heard, "Nice shoes." He looked around, and didn't see anyone nearby.

Then he heard, "Great tie!" There was still no one near him. Then he heard, "I like your hat!" Finally he called the waiter over and asked him what was going on.

The waiter said, "Oh, the peanuts are complimentary."

* * *

One guy who won a gold medal at the Olympics liked it so much that he decided to get it bronzed.

* * *

A man was walking down a dark street at night, when he heard a "bump, bump, bump." He turned and saw an upright coffin bumping down the street behind him. He got scared and ran for his house and locked the door. Suddenly the coffin crashed right through the door. Terrified, the man ran up the stairs and into the bathroom, locking the door. A few seconds later, the coffin crashed into the door and broke it down. The man screamed and looked for a weapon to defend himself. He grabbed a bottle of cough syrup and threw it at the coffin. The coffin stopped.

* * *

A social worker who had recently transferred from the big city to the mountains was touring her new territory. She came upon the tiniest cabin she had ever seen. Intrigued, she knocked on the door.

"Anybody home?"

A child's voice answered, "Yep."

"Is your father there?"

"Pa? Nope, he left before Ma came in."

"Well, is your mother there?"

"Nope, Ma left just before I got here."

"Are you never together as a family?"

"Sure, but not here. This is the outhouse!"

* * *

Bubba was bragging to his boss one day. "I know everyone there is to know. Just name someone, anyone, and I know them."

Tired of his boasting, his boss called his bluff. "OK, Bubba, how about Tom Cruise?"

"Sure, yes, Tom and I are old friends, and I can prove it." So Bubba and his boss flew out to Hollywood and knocked on Tom Cruise's door, and sure enough, Tom Cruise shouted, "Bubba! Great to see you! You and your friend come right in and join me for lunch!"

Although impressed, Bubba's boss was still skeptical. After they left Cruise's house, he told Bubba that he thought Bubba's knowing Cruise was just lucky.

"No, no, just name anyone else," Bubba said.

"The President of the United States," his boss quickly retorted.

"Yes," Bubba said, "I know him. Let's fly to Washington."

And off they went. At the White House, the President spotted Bubba on the tour and motioned him and his boss over, saying, "Bubba, what a surprise, I was just on my way to a meeting, but you and your friend come on in and let's have a cup of coffee first and catch up." Well, the boss was very shaken by now, but still not totally convinced.

After they left the White House grounds, he expressed his doubts to Bubba, who again implored him to name anyone else.

"The Pope," his boss replied. "Sure!" said Bubba. "I've known the Pope a long time."

So off they flew to Rome. Bubba and his boss were assembled with the masses in Vatican Square when Bubba said, "This will never work. I can't catch the Pope's eye among all these people. Tell you what, I know all the guards so let me just go upstairs and I'll come out on the balcony with the Pope." And he disappeared into the crowd headed toward the Vatican. Sure enough, half an hour later Bubba emerged with the Pope on the balcony. But by the time Bubba returned, he found that his boss had had a heart attack and was surrounded by paramedics.

Working his way to his boss' side, Bubba asked him, "What happened?"

His boss looked up and said, "I was doing fine until you and the Pope came out on the balcony and the man next to me said, 'Who's that on the balcony with Bubba?'"

*   *   *

Two hillbillies walk into a bar. As they enjoy some refreshment, a woman at a nearby table, who is eating a sandwich, begins to cough. After a minute or so, it becomes apparent that she is in real distress.

One of the hillbillies looks at her and says, "Kin ya swallar?" The woman shakes her head no. "Kin ya breathe?" The woman begins to turn blue and shakes her head no.

The hillbilly walks over to the woman, lifts up the back of her dress, yanks down her drawers and quickly gives her right butt cheek a lick with his tongue. The woman is so shocked that she has a violent spasm and the obstruction flies out of her mouth.

As she begins to breathe again, the hillbilly walks back to the bar. His partner says, "Ya know, I'd heerd of that there 'HindLick Maneuver', but I ain't never seed nobody do it!"

* * *

Three statisticians went deer hunting with bows and arrows. They spotted a big buck and took aim. One shot, and his arrow flew off ten feet to the left. The second shot, and his arrow went ten feet to the right. The third statistician jumped up and down yelling, "We got him! We got him!"

* * *

It was autumn, and the Indians on the remote reservation asked their new Chief if the winter was going to be cold or mild. Since he was an Indian Chief in a modern society, he had never been taught the old secrets. When he looked at the sky, he couldn't tell what the weather was going to be. Nevertheless, to be on the safe side, he replied to his tribe that the winter was indeed going to be cold and that the members of the village should collect firewood to be prepared.

Being a practical leader, after several days he got an idea. He picked up a phone, called the National Weather Service, and asked, "Is the coming winter going to be cold?"

"It looks like this winter is going to be quite cold indeed," the meteorologist at the weather service responded. So the Chief went back to his people and told them to collect even more wood in order to be prepared.

A week later, he called the National Weather Service again. "Is it going to be a very cold winter?"

"Yes," the man at National Weather Service again replied, "it's definitely going to be a very cold winter." The Chief again went back to his people and ordered them to collect every scrap of wood they could find.

Two weeks later, he called the National Weather Service again. "Are you absolutely sure that the winter is going to be very cold?"

"Absolutely," the man replied. "It's going to be one of the coldest winters ever."

"How can you be so sure?" the Chief asked.

The weather man replied, "The Indians are collecting wood like crazy."

* * *

A very dirty little boy came in from playing in the yard and asked his mother, "Who am I?"

Ready to play the game she said, "I don't know! Who are you?"

"Wow!" cried the child. "Mrs. Johnson was right! She said I was so dirty, my own mother wouldn't recognize me!"

* * *

Two cannibals were eating a clown. One said to the other, "Does this taste funny to you?"

* * *

Sid and Al were sitting in a Chinese restaurant. "Sid," asked Al, "I wonder if there are any Jews in China?"

"I don't know," Sid replied. "Why don't we ask the waiter?"

When the waiter came by, Al asked him, "Do you have any Chinese Jews in China?"

"I don't know, sir, let me ask," the waiter replied, and he went into the kitchen. He returned in a few minutes and said, "No sir, no Chinese Jews."

"Are you sure?" Al asked.

"I will check again, sir," the waiter replied and went back to the kitchen.

While he was still gone, Sid said, "I cannot believe there are no Jews in China. Our people are scattered everywhere."

When the waiter returned, he said, "Sir, no Chinese Jews."

"Are you really sure?" Al asked again. "I cannot believe there are no Chinese Jews."

"Sir, I ask everyone in kitchen," the waiter replied, exasperated. "We have orange Jews, prune Jews, tomato Jews and grape Jews, but no one ever hear of Chinese Jews!"

* * *

A termite walked into a bar and said, "Is the bar tender here?"

*   *   *

A man walked into a bar with a piece of tarmac under his arm and placed it gently on the stool beside him. He said, "I'll have a drink please, and one for the road."

*   *   *

Two cannibals were eating dinner. One said, "I really hate my mother-in-law."

The other said, "Well, just eat the noodles."

*   *   *

"How was your date last night?"

"Fabulous. We went to the concert, had a bite to eat, and then we drove around for a while until I found a nice spot to park overlooking the city lights. I asked her for a kiss, and she said that first I'd have to put the top down on the car. So I worked for an hour getting the top down—"

"An hour? I can put my top down in three minutes."

"I know. But you have a convertible."

*   *   *

A man went into a restaurant called "The Moon." The food was good, but there was no atmosphere.

*   *   *

A beggar walked up to a well-dressed woman shopping on Rodeo Drive and said, "I haven't eaten anything in four days."

She looked at him and said, "Wow, I wish I had your willpower."

*   *   *

A man walks into a restaurant with an ostrich behind him, and as he sits, the waitress comes over and asks for their order. The man says, "I'll have a hamburger, fries and a coke," and turns to the ostrich. "What's yours?" "I'll have the same," says the ostrich.

A short time later the waitress returns with the order. "That will be $6.40 please," and the man reaches into his pocket and pulls out exact change for payment.

The next day, the man and the ostrich come again and the man says, "I'll have a hamburger, fries and a coke," and the ostrich says, "I'll have the same." Once again the man reaches into his pocket and pays with exact change.

This becomes a routine until late one evening the two enter again. "The usual?" asks the waitress. "No, this is Friday night, so I'll have a steak, baked potato and salad," says the man. "Same for me," says the ostrich.

A short time later the waitress comes with the order and says, "That will be $12.62." Once again the man pulls exact change out of his pocket and places it on the table.

The waitress can't hold back her curiosity any longer. "Excuse me, sir. How do you manage to always come up with the exact change out of your pocket every time?"

"Well," says the man, "several years ago I was cleaning the attic and I found an old lamp. When I rubbed it a genie appeared and offered me two wishes. My first wish was that if I ever had to pay for anything, I could just put my hand in my pocket, and the right amount of money would always be there."

"That's brilliant!" says the waitress. "Most people would wish for a million dollars or something, but you'll always be as rich as you want for as long as you live!"

"That's right," he says, "whether it's a gallon of milk or a Rolls Royce, the exact money is always there."

The waitress asks, "One other thing, sir, what's with the ostrich?"

"My second wish was for a chick with long legs."

*   *   *

When Mozart passed away, he was buried in a churchyard. A couple days later, the town drunk was walking through the cemetery and heard some strange noise coming from the area where Mozart was buried. Terrified, the drunk ran and got the priest to come and listen to it. The priest bent close to the grave and heard some faint, unrecognizable music coming from the grave.

Frightened, the priest ran and got the town magistrate. When the magistrate arrived, he bent his ear to the grave, listened for a moment, and said, "Ah, yes, that's Mozart's Ninth Symphony, being played backwards."

He listened a while longer, and said, "There's the Eighth Symphony, and it's backwards, too. Most puzzling." So the magistrate kept listening. "There's the Seventh . . . the Sixth . . . the Fifth . . ." Suddenly the realization of what was happening dawned on the magistrate. He stood up and announced to the crowd that had gathered in the cemetery, "My fellow citizens, there's nothing to worry about. It's just Mozart decomposing."

* * *

Little Johnny came into the house with a new harmonica. "Grandpa, do you mind if I play this in here?"

"Of course not, Johnny. I love music. In fact, when your grandma and I were young, music saved my life."

"What happened?"

"Well, it was during the famous Johnstown flood. The dam broke, and when the water hit our house, it knocked it right off the foundation. Grandma got on the dining room table and floated out safely."

"How about you?"

"Me? I accompanied her on the piano!"

* * *

A neutron walked into a bar and asked the bartender, "How much for a drink?"

The bartender said, "For you, no charge."

* * *

When Rufus accidentally lost 50 cents in the outhouse, he immediately threw in his watch and billfold. He explained, "I'm not going down there just for 50 cents."

* * *

Two guys are driving through Alabama when they get pulled over by a state trooper. The trooper walks up and taps on the window with his nightstick. The driver rolls down the window, and the trooper smacks him in the head with the stick.

The driver says, "Why'd you do that?"

The trooper says, "You're in Alabama, son. When I pull you over, you have your license ready."

The driver says, "I'm sorry, officer, I'm not from around here."

The trooper runs a check on the guy's license, and he's clean. He gives the guy his license back and walks around to the passenger side and taps on the window. The passenger rolls his window down, and the trooper smacks him with the nightstick.

The passenger says, "What'd you do that for?"

The cop says, "Just making your wish come true."

The passenger says, "Huh?"

The cop says, "I know that two miles down the road you're gonna say, 'I sure wish that moron would've tried that stuff with me.'"

*　*　*

Two cannibals walked into a bar in Prague and asked for separate Czechs.

*　*　*

I was about six, and I was playing one day, and I saw the cellar door open, just a crack. Now ever since I could remember, my parents had always told me, "Elmo, whatever you do . . . don't go near the cellar door." But I had to see what was on the other side, even if it killed me. So I went to the cellar door, and I pushed it open and walked through, and I saw strange, wonderful things, things I had never seen before, like trees, grass, flowers, the sun . . ."

*　*　*

A couple of rednecks were out in the woods hunting when one of them suddenly grabbed his chest and fell to the ground. He didn't seem to be breathing;

145

his eyes were rolled back in his head. The other redneck whipped out his cell phone and called 911.

He gasped to the operator, "I think Bubba is dead! What should I do?"

The operator, in a calm soothing voice, said, "Just take it easy and follow my instructions. First, let's make sure he's dead."

There was silence . . . then a shot was heard.

The redneck's voice came back on the line. "Okay, now what?"

*   *   *

My luck is so bad that if I bought a cemetery, people would stop dying.

*   *   *

The first time I got a universal remote control, I thought to myself, "This changes everything."

*   *   *

At a golf course, four men approached the sixteenth tee. The straight fairway ran along a road and bike path on the left. The first golfer teed off and hooked the ball, which bounced off the bike path onto the road and then hit the tire of a moving bus and was knocked back onto the fairway.

As they all stood in silent amazement, one man finally asked him, "How on earth did you do that?"

He shrugged and said, "You have to know the bus schedule."

*   *   *

For a moment, nothing happened. Then, after a second or so, nothing continued to happen.

*   *   *

One beautiful December evening Pedro and his girlfriend Rosita were sitting by the side of the ocean. There was a romantic full moon, and Pedro said, "Hey, Rosita, let's play Weeweechu."

"Oh no, not now, let's look at the moon," said Rosita.

"Oh, c'mon baby, let's you and I play Weeweechu. I love you and it's the perfect time," Pedro begged.

"But I wanna just hold your hand and watch the moon."

"Please, corazoncita, just once, play Weeweechu with me."

Rosita looked at Pedro and said, "OK, one time, we'll play Weeweechu."

Pedro grabbed his guitar and they both sang, "Weeweechu a Merry Christmas, Weeweechu a Merry Christmas, Weeweechu a Merry Christmas, and a Happy New Year."

* * *

Someone knocked on my door and asked for a small donation towards the local swimming pool. I gave them a glass of water.

* * *

Two trucks loaded with a thousand copies of *Roget's Thesaurus* collided as they left a New York publishing house last Thursday, according to the Associated Press. Witnesses were stunned, startled, aghast, taken aback, stupefied, amazed, astounded, and unsettled.

* * *

Two rednecks were out hunting, and as they were walking along they saw a huge hole in the ground. They approached it and were amazed by the size of it. The first hunter said, "Wow, that's some hole. I can't even see the bottom. Wonder how deep it is."

The second hunter said, "I don't know. Let's throw something down and listen and see how long it takes to hit bottom."

The first hunter said, "There's this old transmission here. Give me a hand and we'll throw it in and see."

So they picked it up and carried it over and threw it in the hole. They were standing there listening and looking over the edge and they heard a rustling in the brush behind them. As they turned around, they saw a goat come crashing through the brush, run up to the hole, and with no hesitation, go in headfirst.

While they were standing there looking at each other and looking in the hole, and trying to figure out what that was all about, an old farmer walked up. "Say there," said the farmer, "you fellers didn't happen to see my goat around here anywhere, did you?"

The first hunter said, "Funny you should ask, but we were just standing here a minute ago and a goat came running out of the bushes doin' about a hunert miles an hour and jumped headfirst into this hole here!"

And the old farmer said, "Why that's impossible. I had him chained to an old transmission!"

* * *

An artist was asked by the Seventh Cavalry to do a painting of General Custer's last thoughts. The artist drew a pastoral scene with a large cow in the foreground and thousands of Indians surrounding it. Curiously, the cow had several large holes in its side. The caption read, as Custer might have phrased it, "Holy cow! Look at all those Indians!"

* * *

A lawyer walked into a bar and sat down next to a drunk who was closely examining something held in his fingers. The lawyer watched the drunk for a while till he finally got curious enough to ask what it was.

"Well," said the drunk, "it looks like plastic and feels like rubber."

"Let me have it," said the lawyer. Taking it, he began to roll it between his thumb and forefinger, examining it closely. "Yes," he finally said, "it does look like plastic and feel like rubber, but I don't know what it is. Where did you get it?"

"From my nose," the drunk replied.

* * *

King Ozymandias was running low on cash after years of war with the Hittites. His last great possession was the Star of the Euphrates, the most valuable diamond in the ancient world. Desperate, he went to Crosus, the pawnbroker, to get a loan.

Crosus said, "I'll give you 100,000 dinars for it."

"But I paid a million dinars for it," the king protested. "Don't you know who I am? I am the king!"

Crosus replied, "When you wish to pawn a Star, makes no difference who you are."

* * *

"What's the quickest way from here to Philadelphia?"

"Are you walking or driving?"

"I'm driving."

"That's definitely the quickest way."

* * *

Two American tourists were driving through Wales. They decided to stop for lunch in the village of Llanfairpwllgwyngyllgery-chwyrndrobwllllantysiliogogoch. Baffled by the name, one of them turned to a local man and asked, "Would you please say where we are—very slowly?"

The Welshman leaned over and said, very slowly, "Burrr-gerrr Kinngg."

* * *

Little Johnny was celebrating his birthday soon. His father asked him what he would like for his birthday. Without hesitation Johnny said, "A spider." His father was somewhat incredulous, so he asked him again. "I really want a spider," Johnny replied.

His father went to the pet store and asked the salesperson, "Do you sell spiders?"

"We sure do," was the response.

"How much do they cost?"

"$50.00," said the clerk.

Johnny's father said, "That's too expensive. I'm sure I can find something cheaper on the web."

* * *

The policeman got out of his car as the teenager who was stopped for speeding rolled down his window. "I've been waiting for you all day," said the officer.

The young man replied, "Well, I got here as fast as I could."

*   *   *

A Scandinavian couple went to the Olympics. While they were watching the track and field competition, a lady turned to the man and said, "Are you a pole vaulter?"

He said, "No, I'm Norvegian, and my name isn't Valter."

*   *   *

I heard about a guy who was hosting a party and made his guests line up for juice. I don't remember the rest of the story, except that there was a really long punch line.

*   *   *

Famous first lines of bad novels

1. "Although Bekka had an abnormal fear of mice, it did not keep her from eeking out a living at a local pet store."

2. "As a scientist, Johnson knew that if he were ever to break wind in the echo chamber he would never hear the end of it."

*   *   *

Punny Stuff

She had a boyfriend with a wooden leg, but broke it off.

People who jump off a Paris bridge are in Seine.

If you don't pay your exorcist, you get repossessed.

He often broke into song because he couldn't find the key.

When the plums dry on your tree, it's time to prune.

Pigs who play basketball are ball-hogs.

*   *   *

New Word Definitions

Reintarnation: Coming back to life as a hillbilly.

Giraffiti: Vandalism spray-painted very, very high.

Inoculatte: To take coffee intravenously when you are running late.

Osteopornosis: A degenerate disease.

Dopeler effect: The tendency of stupid ideas to seem smarter when they come to you rapidly.

Arachnoleptic fit: The frantic dance performed just after you've accidently walked through a spider web.

Beelzebug: Satan in the form of a mosquito that gets into your bedroom at three in the morning and cannot be cast out.

Lawyers and Weird Stuff

A seven-year-old boy was at the center of a courtroom drama when he challenged a court ruling over who should have custody of him. The boy has a history of being beaten by his parents, and the judge awarded custody to his aunt. The boy confirmed that his aunt beat him more than his parents and refused to live there. When the judge suggested that he live with his grandparents, the boy cried out that they beat him more than anyone. So the judge allowed the boy to choose who should have custody of him. Custody was granted to the Baltimore Orioles this morning as the boy firmly believes that they are not capable of beating anyone.

* * *

Taking his seat in his chambers, the judge faced the opposing lawyers. "So," he said, "I have been presented, by both of you, with a bribe."

Both lawyers squirmed uncomfortably. "You, attorney Jones, gave me $15,000. And you, attorney Smith, gave me $10,000." The judge reached into his pocket, pulled out a check, and handed it to Jones. "Now then, I'm returning $5,000, and we're going to decide this case solely on its merits!"

* * *

One afternoon, a wealthy lawyer was riding in the back of his limousine when he saw two men eating grass by the road side. He ordered his driver to stop and he got out to investigate.

"Why are you eating grass?" he asked one man.

"We don't have any money for food," the poor man replied.

"Oh, come along with me then."

"But sir, I have a wife with two children!"

"Bring them along! And you, come with us too!" he said to the other man.

"But sir, I have a wife with six children!" the second man answered.

"Bring them as well!"

They all climbed into the car, which was no easy task, even for a car as large as the limo. Once underway, one of the poor fellows said, "Sir, you are too kind. Thank you for taking all of us with you."

The lawyer replied, "No problem; the grass at my home is about two feet tall!"

* * *

A defendant was on trial for murder. There was strong evidence indicating guilt, but there was no corpse. In the defense's closing statement the lawyer, knowing that his client would probably be convicted, resorted to a trick.

"Ladies and gentlemen of the jury, I have a surprise for you all," the lawyer said as he looked at his watch. "Within one minute, the person presumed dead in this case will walk into this courtroom." He looked toward the court-room door. The jurors, somewhat stunned, all looked on eagerly. A minute passed. Nothing happened.

Finally the lawyer said, "Actually, I made up the previous statement. But, you all looked on with anticipation. I therefore put to you that you have a reason-able doubt in this case as to whether anyone was killed and insist that you return a verdict of not guilty." The jury, clearly confused, retired to deliberate. A few minutes later, the jury returned and pronounced a verdict of guilty.

"But how?" inquired the lawyer. "You must have had some doubt. I saw all of you stare at the door."

The jury foreman replied, "Oh, we looked, but your client didn't."

* * *

A man was sued by a woman for defamation of character. She charged that he had called her a pig. The man was found guilty and fined. After the trial he asked the judge, "This means that I cannot call Mrs. Johnson a pig?"

The judge said that was true. "Does this mean I cannot call a pig Mrs. Johnson?" the man asked.

The judge replied that he could indeed call a pig Mrs. Johnson with no fear of legal action.

The man looked directly at Mrs. Johnson and said, "Good afternoon, Mrs. Johnson."

*   *   *

If you're pulled over by a policeman and he says, "Your eyes look red. Have you been drinking?" you probably shouldn't respond, "Gee, Officer, your eyes look glazed. Have you been eating doughnuts?"

*   *   *

Apparently, 1 in 5 people in the world are Chinese. And there are 5 people in my family, so it must be one of them. It's either my mom or my dad. Or my older brother Colin. Or my younger brother Ho Cha Chu.

But I think it's Colin.

*   *   *

Every day I beat my own previous record for number of consecutive days I've stayed alive.

*   *   *

Life is like a dog-sled team. If you ain't the lead dog, the scenery never changes.

*   *   *

I have finally developed a static aerobic exercise program that works. It only takes several minutes, three days a week. I started by standing in my kitchen with a 5-pound potato sack in each hand. I extended my arms straight out to my sides and held them there long as I could. At first it was only for several seconds before my arms fatigued.

After a few weeks I moved up to 10-pound potato sacks, then 50-pound potato sacks, and finally I got to where I could lift a 100-pound potato sack in each hand and hold my arms straight out for more than a full minute!

Next, I started putting a potato into each of the sacks, but I caution you not to overdo it at this level.

*   *   *

A tour guide was showing a tourist around Washington, D.C. The guide pointed out the place where George Washington supposedly threw a dollar across the Potomac River.

"That's impossible," said the tourist. "No one could throw a coin that far!"

"You have to remember," answered the guide. "A dollar went a lot farther in those days."

* * *

If you're gonna get a tattoo, just get one: the words, "I'm dumb." That's it. That way in 10 years, when you go, "Why did I get this?" you'll already have the answer.

* * *

Before you criticize someone, you should walk a mile in their shoes. That way, when you criticize them, you're a mile away and you have their shoes.

* * *

Research shows that six out of seven dwarfs aren't Happy.

* * *

A certain jungle tribe lived in grass huts in a small village. Their most prized possession was a golden throne that sat in the chief's house. One day a nearby tribe attacked and threatened to overrun the village. The chief decided to hide the throne in his attic. When the attackers started shooting flaming arrows, one of them struck the chief's house and its roof began to burn. A few minutes later, as the chief was conferring with his generals on their defense strategy, the heavy golden throne sank through the burning attic floor and crashed down on the chief, killing him instantly. The moral: People who live in grass houses shouldn't stow thrones.

* * *

Do not argue with an idiot. He will drag you down to his level and beat you with experience.

* * *

By the time a man is wise enough to watch his step, he's too old to go anywhere.

* * *

After eating an entire bull, a mountain lion felt so good he started roaring. He kept it up until a hunter came along and shot him.

The moral: When you're full of bull, keep your mouth shut!

*   *   *

ATTORNEY: How old is your son, the one living with you?

WITNESS: Thirty-eight or thirty-five, I can't remember which.

ATTORNEY: How long has he lived with you?

WITNESS: Forty-five years.

*   *   *

ATTORNEY: This *myasthenia gravis*, does it affect your memory at all?

WITNESS: Yes.

ATTORNEY: And in what ways does it affect your memory?

WITNESS: I forget.

ATTORNEY: You forget? Can you give us an example of something you forgot?

*   *   *

ATTORNEY: She had three children, right?

WITNESS: Yes.

ATTORNEY: How many were boys?

WITNESS: None.

ATTORNEY: Were there any girls?

WITNESS: Your Honor, I need a different attorney. Can I get a new attorney?

*   *   *

ATTORNEY: How was your first marriage terminated?

WITNESS: By death.

ATTORNEY: And by whose death was it terminated?

WITNESS: Take a guess.

*   *   *

ATTORNEY: Doctor, how many of your autopsies have you performed on dead people?

WITNESS: All of them. The live ones put up too much of a fight.

*   *   *

ATTORNEY: Do you recall the time that you examined the body?

WITNESS: The autopsy started around 8:30 PM.

ATTORNEY: And Mr. Denton was dead at the time?

WITNESS: If not, he was by the time I finished.

*   *   *

ATTORNEY: Doctor, before you performed the autopsy, did you check for a pulse?

WITNESS: No.

ATTORNEY: Did you check for blood pressure?

WITNESS: No.

ATTORNEY: Did you check for breathing?

WITNESS: No.

ATTORNEY: So, then, it is possible that the patient was alive when you began the autopsy?

WITNESS: No.

ATTORNEY: How can you be so sure, Doctor?

WITNESS: Because his brain was sitting on my desk in a jar.

ATTORNEY: I see, but could the patient have still been alive, nevertheless?

WITNESS: Yes, it is possible that he could have been alive and practicing law.

*   *   *

A Mexican bandit made a specialty of crossing the Rio Grande from time to time and robbing banks in Texas. Finally, a reward was offered for his capture, and an enterprising Texas ranger decided to track him down.

After a lengthy search, he traced the bandit to his favorite cantina, snuck up behind him, put his trusty six-shooter to the bandit's head, and said, "You're under arrest. Tell me where you hid the loot or I'll blow your brains out." But the bandit didn't speak English, and the Ranger didn't speak Spanish.

Fortunately, a bilingual lawyer was in the saloon and translated the Ranger's message. The terrified bandit blurted out, in Spanish, that the loot was buried under the oak tree in back of the cantina.

"What did he say?" asked the Ranger.

The lawyer answered, "He said, 'Get lost, Gringo. You wouldn't dare shoot me.'"

* * *

Whoever invented Knock-Knock jokes should be given the "no-bell" prize.

* * *

You May Be A Redneck:

* If you take your dog for a walk and you both use the same tree.

* If you come back from the dump with more than you took.

* If your wife can climb a tree faster than your cat.

* If you've ever been kicked out of the zoo for heckling the monkeys.

* If you wonder how service stations keep their restrooms so clean.

* If you sit on your roof at Christmas time hoping to fill your deer quota.

* * *

Arbitrator – a cook that leaves Arby's to work at McDonald's.

Avoidable – what a bullfighter tries to do.

Burglarize – what a crook sees with.

Counterfeiters – workers who put together kitchen cabinets.

Eclipse – what an English barber does for a living.

Eyedropper – a clumsy ophthalmologist.

Misty – how some golfers create divots.

Relief – what trees do in the spring.

Rubberneck – what you do to relax your wife.

Selfish – what the owner of a seafood store does.

Subdued – like, a guy, like, works on one of those, like, submarines, man.

Working for the Man

A new high school graduate decided to join the circus for the summer. Because of his slim physique, they made him the "human cannon-ball." Three times a day, he was shot out of a cannon from one end of the big top to the other, landing safely in a net. At the end of the summer, he reminded his boss that he was quitting in order to start college. The circus owner came and begged him to stay on, saying, "We'll never find another man of your caliber!"

* * *

A crow was sitting in a tree, doing nothing all day. A small rabbit saw the crow, and asked him, "Can I also sit like you and do nothing all day?"

The crow answered, "Sure, why not?" So the rabbit sat on the ground below the crow, and rested. All of a sudden, a fox appeared, jumped on the rabbit, and ate it.

The moral to the story is: To be sitting and doing nothing, you must be sitting very, very high up.

* * *

Judge: Is there any reason you could not serve as a juror in this case?

Juror: I don't want to be away from my job that long.

Judge: Can't they do without you at work?

Juror: Yes, but I don't want them to know it.

* * *

"Do you believe in life after death?" the boss asked one of his employees.

"Yes, sir," the new employee replied.

"Well, then, that makes everything just fine," the boss went on. "After you left early yesterday to go to your grandmother's funeral, she stopped in to see you!"

* * *

A guy stopped at a local gas station and, after filling his tank, he paid the bill and bought a soft drink. He stood by his car to drink his cola and watched a couple of men working along the roadside. One man would dig a hole two or three feet deep and then move on. The other man came along behind him and filled in the hole. While one was digging a new hole, the other was 25 feet behind filling in the hole. The men worked right past the guy with the soft drink and went on down the road.

"I can't stand this," said the man, tossing the can into a trash container and heading down the road toward the men. "Hold it, hold it," he said to the men. "Can you tell me what's going on here with all this digging and refilling?"

"Well, we work for the government and we're just doing our job," one of the men said.

"But one of you is digging a hole and the other fills it up. You're not accomplishing anything. Aren't you wasting the taxpayers' money?"

"You don't understand, mister," one of the men said, leaning on his shovel and wiping his brow. "Normally there's three of us: me, Elmer and Leroy. I dig the hole, Elmer sticks in the tree, and Leroy, here, puts the dirt back. Now just because Elmer's sick, that don't mean that Leroy and me can't work."

* * *

Once upon a time the government had a vast scrap yard in the middle of a desert. Congress said someone may steal from it at night, so they created a night watchman GS-4 position and hired a person for the job.

Then Congress said, "How does the watchman do his job without instruction?" So they created a planning position and hired two people, one person to write the instructions, a GS-12, and one person to do time studies, a GS-11. Then Congress said, "How will we know the night watchman is doing the tasks correctly?"

So they created a Quality Control position and hired two people, one GS-9 to do the studies and one GS-11 to write the reports. Then Congress said, "How are these people going to get paid?" So they created the following positions: a time keeper, GS-09, and a payroll officer, GS-11, and hired two people.

Then Congress said, "Who will be accountable for all of these people?" So they created an administrative position and hired three people: an Admin. Officer GS-13, Assistant Admin. Officer GS-12, and a Legal Secretary GS-08.

Then Congress said, "We have had this command in operation for one year and we are $18,000 over budget. We must cut back the overall cost."

So they laid off the night watchman.

* * *

Reaching the end of a job interview, the human resources person asked a young engineer fresh out of MIT what kind of a salary he was looking for.

"In the neighborhood of $200,000 a year, depending on the benefits package."

"Well, what would you say to a package of 5-weeks vacation, 14 paid holidays, full medical and dental, company matching retirement fund to 50% of salary, and a company car leased every 2 years . . . say, a red Corvette?"

"Wow! Are you kidding?"

"Yeah, but you started it."

* * *

A young lad asked an old man how he became so rich. The old man replied, "Well, son, it was 1932 and the depth of the Great Depression. I was down to my last nickel, so I invested it in an apple. I spent an entire day polishing that apple and at the end of the day, I sold it for a dime. So the next day I bought two apples. I polished them all day and sold them at the end of the day for two dimes. I continued doing this for a month, and by the end of that month, I had accumulated a total, minus expenses of course, of $4.00."

"And then what?" the lad asked.

"Then my wife's father died and left us two million dollars!"

* * *

A really huge muscular guy with a bad stutter walked into a department store and asked, "W-w-w-where's the m-m-m-men's dep-p-p-partment?"

The clerk behind the counter just looked at him and said nothing.

The man repeated himself: "W-w-w-where's the m-m-m-men's dep-p-p-partment?"

Again, the clerk didn't answer him.

The guy asked several more times: "W-w-w-where's the m-m-m-men's dep-p-p-partment?"

And the clerk just seemed to ignore him.

Finally, the guy stormed off in anger.

The customer who was waiting in line behind the guy asked the clerk, "Why wouldn't you answer that guy's question?"

The clerk answered, "D-d-d-do you th-th-th-think I w-w-w-want to get b-b-b-beat up?!!"

* * *

Suzy couldn't believe it when she got fired from the calendar factory. All she did was take a day off.

* * *

Although he was a qualified meteorologist, Hopkins ran up a terrible record of forecasting for the TV news program. He became something of a local joke when a newspaper began keeping a record of his predictions and showed that he'd been wrong almost three hundred times in a single year.

That kind of notoriety was enough to get him fired.

He moved to another part of the country and applied for a similar job. One blank on the job application called for the reason for leaving his previous position.

Hopkins wrote, "The climate didn't agree with me."

* * *

A lady threw a party for her granddaughter. She had gone all out with a caterer, a band, and even a clown. Just before the party started, two bums showed up looking for a handout. Feeling sorry for the bums, the woman told them that she would give them a meal if they would chop some wood for her out back. Gratefully, they headed to the rear of the house.

The guests arrived, and all was going well with the children having a wonderful time. But the clown hadn't shown up. After a half an hour, the clown finally called to report that he was stuck in traffic, and he would probably not make the party at all.

The woman was very disappointed and unsuccessfully tried to entertain the children herself. She happened to look out the window and saw one of the bums doing cartwheels across the lawn. She watched in awe as he swung from tree branches, did midair flips, and leaped high into the air.

She spoke to the other bum and said, "What your friend is doing is absolutely marvelous. I've never seen such a thing. Do you think your friend would consider repeating this performance for the children at the party? I would pay him $100!"

The other bum said, "Well, I dunno. Let me ask him. Hey Willie! For $100, would you chop off another toe?"

* * *

A group of managers is trying to calculate the height of a flag pole. They try to measure its height by lining up their thumbs and then turning the thumb 90 degrees and marking a spot on the ground. Then they try to use its shadow and trig functions, but with no luck.

An engineer comes by and watches for a few minutes. He asks one of the managers what they're doing.

"We're trying to calculate the height of this flag pole."

The engineer watches a few minutes more and then, without saying a word, he walks over, pulls the pole out of the ground, lays it down, measures it, writes the measurement on a piece of paper, gives it to one of the managers, and walks away.

The manager looks at the paper, snickers and says to the other managers: "Isn't that just like an engineer? We're trying to calculate the height and he gives us the length."

* * *

A fire started in some grass on a farm. The county fire department was called to put out the blaze. But the fire was more than the county could handle.

Someone suggested that a nearby volunteer group be called. Despite some doubts, the call was made.

The volunteers arrived in a dilapidated old fire truck. They rumbled straight toward the fire, drove right into the middle of the flames and stopped! The firemen jumped off the truck and frantically started spraying water in all directions. Soon they had snuffed out the center of the fire, breaking the blaze into two easily controlled parts.

Watching all this, the farmer was so impressed with the volunteer department's work and so grateful that his farm had been spared, that on the spot he presented the volunteers with a check for $1,000. A local news reporter asked the volunteer fire captain what the department planned to do with the funds. "That ought to be obvious," he responded, wiping ashes off his coat. "We're gonna get the brakes fixed on that fire truck!"

* * *

A man in a blue suit had fallen between the rails in a subway station. People were all crowding around, vainly trying to get him out before the train ran him over. Everyone was shouting, "Give me your hand!" Alas, the man would not reach up.

Suddenly, Ben Bebo, the wise guru, elbowed his way through the crowd and leaned over the man.

"Friend," he asked with compassion, "what is your profession?"

"I am an income tax inspector," gasped the man in the blue suit.

"Please, sir, take my hand," said Ben Bebo.

The man immediately grasped the guru's hand and was quickly pulled to safety. Ben Bebo then turned to the amazed bystanders and said, "Never ask a tax man to 'give' you anything, my friends."

* * *

A local United Way office realized that it had never received a donation from the town's most successful lawyer. The person in charge of contributions called him to persuade him to contribute. "Our research shows that out of a yearly income of at least $500,000, you give not a penny to charity. Wouldn't you like to give back to the community in some way?"

The lawyer mulled this over for a moment and replied, "First, did your research also show that my mother is dying after a long illness, and has medical bills that are several times her annual income?"

Embarrassed, the caller mumbled, "Um . . . no."

"Or that my brother, a disabled veteran, is blind and confined to a wheelchair?"

The stricken representative began to stammer out an apology but was interrupted. "Or that my sister's husband died in a traffic accident," said the lawyer, his voice rising in indignation, "leaving her penniless with three children?"

The humiliated caller, completely beaten, said simply, "I had no idea."

The lawyer cut him off once again. "So if I don't give any money to them, why should I give any to you?!?"

* * *

A father was asked by his friend, "Has your son decided what he wants to be when he grows up?"

"Yes, he wants to be a garbage collector," replied the boy's father.

His friend thought for a moment and responded, "That's a rather strange ambition to have for a career."

"Well," said the boy's father, "he thinks that garbage collectors only work on Tuesdays!"

* * *

A sheriff walked into a saloon and said, "Has anyone seen Brown Paper Jake? He wears a brown paper hat, a brown paper shirt, brown paper boots, brown paper pants, and a brown paper jacket."

The bartender said, "What's he wanted for?"

The sheriff said, "Rustlin."

* * *

"Give me a sentence about a public servant," said a teacher.

The small boy wrote, "The fireman came down the ladder pregnant."

The teacher took the lad aside to correct him. "Do you know what pregnant means?" she asked.

"Sure," said the young boy confidently. "It means carrying a child."

* * *

At a convention of biological scientists, one prominent researcher remarked to another, "Did you know that in our lab we have switched from rats to lawyers for our experiments?"

"Really?" the other researcher replied. "Why did you switch?"

"Well, for three reasons. First, we found that lawyers are far more plentiful. Second, the lab assistants don't get so attached to them. And third, there are some things even a rat won't do."

* * *

I'm great at multitasking. I can waste time, be unproductive, and procrastinate all at once.

* * *

Two factory workers were talking. "I think I'll take some time off from work," said the man.

"How do you think you'll do that?" said the blonde.

He climbed up to the rafters and hung from them upside down. The boss walked in, saw the worker hanging from the ceiling, and asked him what on earth he was doing.

"I'm a light bulb," the guy answered.

"I think you need some time off," said the boss.

So the man jumped down and walked out of the factory.

The blonde began walking out too. The boss asked her where she thought she was going.

The blonde answered, "Home. I can't work in the dark."

* * *

An inter-office softball game was held between the marketing and support staff of one company. The support staff whipped the marketing department soundly.

The marketing staff posted this memo on the bulletin board after the game:

"The Marketing Department is pleased to announce that for the 2019 Softball Season, we came in 2nd place, having lost but one game all year. The Support Department, however, had a rather dismal season, winning only one game."

* * *

Taxiing down the tarmac, the jetliner abruptly stopped, turned around, and returned to the gate. After an hour-long wait, it finally took off.

A concerned passenger asked the flight attendant, "What was the problem?"

"The pilot was bothered by a noise he heard in the engine," explained the flight attendant, "and it took us a while to find a new pilot."

* * *

A trucker came into a truck stop cafe and placed his order. He said, "I want three flat tires, a pair of headlights, and pair of running boards."

The brand-new waitress, not wanting to appear stupid, went to the kitchen and said to the cook, "This guy out there just ordered three flat tires, a pair of headlights, and a pair of running boards. What does he think this place is, an auto parts store?"

"No," the cook said. "Three flat tires mean three pancakes, a pair of headlights is two eggs sunny side up, and running boards are two slices of crisp bacon."

"Oh, OK!" said the waitress. She thought about it for a moment and then spooned up a bowl of beans and gave it to the customer.

The trucker asked, "What are the beans for?"

She replied, "I thought while you were waiting for the flat tires, headlights and running boards, you might as well gas up!"

* * *

"I'm never going to work for that man again."

"Why? What did he say?"

"You're fired!"

*   *   *

One day, the Captain of the 40-oared royal Nile barge went down to speak to the oarsmen in the hold of his ship.

"Men, I have some good news and some bad news. The good news is, the Queen will be joining us today for a trip up the Nile."

The men cheered and sang the praises of the Queen. The captain then continued, "The bad news is, she wants to go water skiing."

*   *   *

The manager of a ladies' dress shop realized it was time to give one of her sales clerks a little talking-to. "Judy, your figures are well below any of our other salespeople's. In fact, unless you can improve your record soon, I'm afraid I'll have to let you go."

"I'm sorry, Ma'am," said a humbled Judy. "Can you give me any advice on how to do better?"

"Well, there is an old trick I can tell you about. It sounds silly, but it's worked for me in the past. Get a dictionary and go through it until you come to a word that has a special power for you. Memorize it, work it into your sales pitch whenever it seems appropriate, and you'll be amazed at the results."

Sure enough, Judy's sales figures went way up, and at the end of the month, the manager called her in again and congratulated her. "Did you try my little trick?" she asked.

Judy nodded. "It took me a whole weekend to find the right word, but I did: 'fantastic.'"

"'Fantastic.' What a good word," said the manager encouragingly. "How've you been using it?"

"Well, my first customer on Monday was a woman who told me her little girl had just been accepted at the most exclusive prep school in the city. I said, 'Fantastic.' She went on to tell me how her daughter always got straight A's and was the most popular girl in her class. I said, 'Fantastic' and she bought $300 worth of clothing. My next customer said she needed a formal dress for the spring ball at the country club, which she was in charge of. I said, 'Fantastic.' She went on to say she had the best figure of anyone on the committee and her husband makes the most money. I said, 'Fantastic,' and she not only bought the designer gown, but hundreds of dollars of other merchandise. It's been like that all week. The customers keep boasting, I keep saying, 'Fantastic,' and they keep buying."

"Excellent work, Judy," complimented her boss. "What did you used to say to customers before you discovered your power word?"

Tina shrugged. "I used to say, 'Who gives a hoot?'"

*   *   *

A man walks into a clock repair shop and the repairman is German and says, "So? Vat sims to be ze problem?"

The man says, "It's my grandfather's clock. It doesn't go 'tick-tock-tick-tock' anymore. Now it just goes 'tick-tick-tick.'"

The repairman replies, "Hmmm! I sink I can fix zis. Let me look inside. Ve haf vays of making you tock!"

*   *   *

Rufus came back to work 15 minutes late. The boss noticed and asked where he had been.

"Getting a haircut."

The boss said, "On company time?"

"It grew on company time."

"Not all of it."

"I didn't get it all cut off."

*   *   *

A movie producer was planning his next blockbuster—an action docudrama about famous composers. So he set up a meeting with Sylvester Stallone, Jean-Claude Van Damme and Arnold Schwarzenegger, and offered them a chance to select which famous musicians they'd portray.

"I've always admired Mozart," Stallone said. "I'd love to play him."

"Chopin has always been my favorite," said Van Damme. "That's the part for me."

The producer turned to Schwarzenegger. "And you, Arnold? Who do you want to be?"

There was a long silence. Then he replied, "I'll be Bach."

* * *

Yesterday a clown opened a door for me. I thought it was a nice jester.

* * *

Three boys were heading home from school when one said, "My dad's way faster than any of yours. He can throw a 90 mph fast ball from the pitcher's mound and run and catch it just after it crosses the plate!"

One of the other boys said, "Oh yeah? Well, my dad can shoot an arrow from his bow and run to the target and hold it up to make sure the arrow hits the bulls-eye!"

The last boy said, "Your dads don't even come close to being faster than mine. My dad works for the government, and even though he works every day until 4:00 he gets home at 3:30!"

* * *

Some guys drove their pickup into a lumberyard. One of them walked into the office and said, "We need some four-by-twos."

The clerk said, "You mean two-by-fours, don't you?"

The man said, "I'll go check," and went back to the truck.

He returned a minute later and said, "Yeah, I meant two-by-fours."

"All right. How long do you need them?" The customer paused for a minute and said, "Uh . . . I'd better go check."

After a while, he returned to the office and said, "A long time. We're gonna build a house."

* * *

My first job was working in an orange juice factory, but I got canned because I couldn't concentrate. Then I worked in the woods as a lumberjack, but I just couldn't hack it, so they gave me the axe. After that I tried to be a tailor, but I just wasn't suited for it. Next I tried working in a muffler factory but that was exhausting. I wanted to be a barber, but I just couldn't cut it. Finally, I attempted to be a deli worker, but any way I sliced it, I couldn't cut the mustard. I studied a long time to become a doctor, but I didn't have any patience. I became a professional fisherman, but discovered that I couldn't live on my net income. Thought about becoming a witch, so I tried that for a spell. I managed to get a good job working for a pool maintenance company, but the work was just too draining. After many years of trying to find steady work, I finally got a job as a historian until I realized there was no future in it.

* * *

A man went into an ice cream parlor and said, "I'd like two scoops of chocolate ice cream, please."

The girl behind the counter said, "I'm very sorry, sir, but our delivery truck broke down this morning. We're out of chocolate."

"In that case," the man said, "I'll have two scoops of chocolate ice cream."

"You don't understand, sir," the girl said. "We have no chocolate."

"Then just give me some chocolate," he said.

Getting angrier by the second, the girl said, "Sir, will you spell VAN, as in vanilla?"

The man said, "V-A-N."

"Now spell STRAW, as in strawberry."

"OK. S-T-R-A-W."

"Now," the girl said, "spell STINK, as in chocolate."

The man hesitated. Then he said, "There is no stink in chocolate."

"THAT'S WHAT I'VE BEEN TRYING TO TELL YOU!" she screamed.

* * *

Preparing for the most important presentation of his life, a sales rep went to a psychiatrist. "I'll implant a hypnotic suggestion in your mind," said the shrink. "Just say 'one-two-three,' and you'll give the best presentation of your life. However, do not say 'one-two-three-four,' because it will cause you to freeze up and make a fool of yourself."

The sales rep was ecstatic. He tried it at home and gave a fabulous presentation. He tried it at work, and got a standing ovation. Then came the big day. Everything was set up in the boardroom and the CEO signaled him to start. The sales rep whispered under his breath, "One-two-three."

Then the CEO asked, "What did you say 'one-two-three' for?"

* * *

Tom was applying for a job as a signalman for the local railroad and was told to meet the inspector at the signal box. The inspector gave Tom a pop quiz: "What would you do if you realized that two trains were heading toward each other on the same track?"

Tom said, "I would switch one train to another track."

"What if the lever broke?" asked the inspector.

"Then I'd run down to the tracks and use the manual lever down there," said Tom.

"What if that had been struck by lightning?" challenged the inspector.

"Then," Tom continued, "I'd run back up here and use the phone to call the next signal box."

"What if the phone was busy?"

"In that case," Tom argued, "I'd run to the street level and use the public phone near the station."

"What if that had been vandalized?"

"Oh well," said Tom, "in that case I would run into town and get my Uncle Leo."

This puzzled the inspector, so he asked, "Why would you do that?"

"Because he's never seen a train crash."

*   *   *

A nursery school teacher was delivering a station wagon full of kids home one day when a fire truck zoomed past. Sitting in the front seat of the fire truck was a Dalmatian dog. The children started discussing the dog's duties.

"They use him to keep crowds back," said one youngster.

"No," said another, "he's just for good luck."

A third child brought the argument to a close. "They use the dogs," she said firmly, "to find the fire hydrant."

*   *   *

A businessman was looking for office help and wanted to be politically correct, so he put a sign in his window stating the following: "HELP WANTED, Must be able to type, must be good with a computer and must be bilingual. We are an Equal Opportunity Employer."

A short time afterwards, a stray dog trotted up to the window of the establishment, saw the sign and went inside. He looked at the receptionist and wagged his tail, then walked over to the sign, looked at it, sat down, and whined.

Getting the idea, the receptionist, who had a good sense of humor, got the businessman, who looked at the stray and was surprised. However, the dog looked determined, so to humor the dog he led it into the office, where upon the dog immediately jumped up on the chair and stared at the man.

The businessman smiled and said, "I can't hire you. The sign says you have to be able to type." The dog jumped down, went to a keyboard and proceeded to type out a perfect business letter. He printed it, trotted over to the businessman and gave it to him, then jumped back on the chair. The businessman was stunned, but then told the dog, "The sign says you have to be good with a computer."

The dog jumped down again and went to the computer. The dog proceeded to demonstrate his expertise with various programs and produced a sample spreadsheet and database and presented them to the businessman. By this time the businessman was totally dumb-founded! He looked at the dog and said, "I realize that you are a very intelligent dog and have some interesting abilities. However, I still can't give you the job."

The dog jumped down and went to a copy of the sign and put his paw on the sentence that stated that he was an "Equal Opportunity Employer." The businessman, getting desperate and looking for a way out, said, "Yes, but the sign also says that you have to be bilingual."

The dog looked him straight in the face and said, "Meow."

* * *

"What's the idea of calling in sick yesterday?"

"I was sick."

"You didn't look sick when I saw you at the racetrack."

"You should have seen me after the sixth race."

* * *

A preacher went to his office on Monday morning and discovered a dead mule in the church yard. He called the police. Since there did not appear to be any foul play, the police referred the preacher to the health department. They said since there was no health threat that he should call the sanitation department. The sanitation manager said he could not pick up the mule without authorization from the mayor.

Now the preacher knew the mayor and was not too eager to call him. The mayor had a bad temper and was generally hard to deal with, but the preacher called him anyway. The mayor immediately began to rant and rave at the pastor and finally said, "Why did you call me anyway? Isn't it your job to bury the dead?"

The preacher paused for a moment, and then said, "Yes, Mayor, it is my job to bury the dead, but I always like to notify the next of kin first!"

* * *

The only thing wrong with a perfect drive to work is that you end up at work.

* * *

The CEO was scheduled to speak at an important convention, so he asked one of his employees to write him a punchy, 20-minute speech. When he returned from the big event, he was furious.

"What's the idea of writing me an hour-long speech?" he demanded to know. "Half the audience walked out before I finished."

The employee was baffled. "I wrote you a 20-minute speech," he replied. "I also gave you the two extra copies you asked for."

*   *   *

A father walked into a market followed by his ten-year-old son. The kid was spinning a quarter in the air and catching it between his teeth. As they walked through the market someone bumped into the boy at just the wrong moment and the coin went straight into his mouth and lodged in his throat. He immediately started choking and going blue in the face and Dad started panicking, shouting and screaming for help.

A middle-aged, unremarkable man in a gray suit was sitting at a coffee bar in the market reading his newspaper and sipping a cup of coffee. At the sound of the commotion he looked up, put his coffee cup down, neatly folded his newspaper and placed it on the counter. He got up from his seat and made his unhurried way across the market. Reaching the boy, the man grabbed him and squeezed gently but firmly. After a few seconds the boy coughed up the quarter, which the man caught in his free hand. The man then walked back to his seat in the coffee bar without saying a word.

As soon as he was sure that his son was fine, the father rushed over to the man and started effusively thanking him. The man looked embarrassed and brushed off the thanks.

As he was about to leave, the father asked one question. "I've never seen any-body do anything like that before. It was fantastic. What are you, a surgeon or something?"

"No," the man replied, "I work for the IRS. Getting people to cough it up is my business."

*   *   *

On a snowy morning, an employee explained why she had arrived for work an hour late. "It was so slippery out there that for every step I took ahead, I slipped back two."

The boss said, "Oh yeah? Then how did you ever get here?"

"I finally gave up," she said, "and started for home."

*   *   *

Did you hear about the director of the DMV who resigned on Tuesday? He tried to resign on Monday, but found he'd been standing in the wrong line.

*   *   *

A customer at a gift shop asked how much they charged to fill balloons with helium. The clerk answered, "It's a quarter per balloon."

She complained, "It used to be ten cents."

Another customer said, "Well, that's inflation."

*   *   *

Three guys were fishing on a lake, and an angel appeared in the boat with them. When the first guy got over his shock, he said to the angel, "I've had back pain for years. Could you please help me?" The angel touched his back, and he felt instant relief.

The second guy pointed to his extra-thick glasses and asked if the angel could cure his poor eyesight. The angel tossed the man's glasses into the lake. When they hit the water, the man's vision cleared and he could see everything distinctly.

The angel turned to the third guy, who threw up his hands in fear. "Don't touch me!" he cried. "I'm on disability!"

*   *   *

A man in the barber shop seemed depressed, so the barber told him, "Cheer up. I knew a guy who owed $5,000 he couldn't pay. He drove his vehicle to the edge of a cliff, where he sat for over an hour. A group of concerned citizens heard about his problem and passed a hat around. Relieved, the man pulled back from the cliff's edge."

"Incredible," said the man. "Who were these kind people?"

"The passengers on the bus."

* * *

On a fully booked airline flight, a passenger stopped the flight attendant and asked, "Is there any way I can get bumped up to first class?"

The attendant shook her head. "Not unless we hit turbulence."

* * *

"I need a raise," the man said to his boss. "There are three other companies after me."

"Is that so?" asked the manager. "What other companies are after you?"

"The electric company, the telephone company, and the gas company."

* * *

The Donald was walking out of the White House and heading toward his limo, when a possible assassin stepped forward and aimed a gun. A secret service agent, new on the job, shouted, "Mickey Mouse!" This startled the would-be assassin, and he was captured.

Later, the secret service agent's supervisor took him aside and asked, "What in the world made you shout Mickey Mouse?"

Blushing, the agent replied, "I got nervous. I meant to shout, 'Donald, duck!'"

* * *

It was a really hot day at the office due to a malfunction with the air conditioning system. There were about twenty people in close quarters and everyone was sweating, even with a fan on. All of a sudden, people started to wrinkle their noses at an odor passing through the air. It was the most hideous smell anyone had ever smelled.

One man, popping his head out of his cubicle, said, "Oh, man! Someone's deodorant isn't working."

A man in the corner replied, "It can't be me. I'm not wearing any."

* * *

The village blacksmith finally found an apprentice willing to work hard for long hours. The blacksmith immediately began his instructions to the lad. "When I take the horseshoe out of the fire, I'll lay it on the anvil. And when I nod my head, you hit it with this hammer."

The apprentice did just as he was told. Now he's the village blacksmith.

* * *

A man was applying for a job as a mechanic. The boss said, "Can you roll your hard hat down your arm and pop it back on your head?" The mechanic nodded.

"Can you play light saber with your wrench and another man's screwdriver?"

"Oh yes," said the mechanic.

"Can you bounce your screwdriver off the cement, grab it, whirl it around and put it in your belt like a gun?"

"Sir, I've been doing that for years!" said the wanna-be mechanic.

"Well in that case, I can't use you. I have 12 men doing that already!" said the boss.

* * *

Police in New Zealand were mystified by the apparent theft of a complete toilet bowl from a police station in Auckland. When a local news reporter asked the sergeant whether they had any leads, he replied, "At present we have nothing to go on."

* * *

A young man, tired of working for others, went into business for himself. Later a friend asked him how he liked being his own boss.

"I don't know," he replied. "The police won't let me park in front of my own business. Tax collectors tell me how to keep books. My banker tells me how much balance I must maintain. Shippers tell me how my goods must be packed. Federal, state, county, and city agencies tell me what records to keep.

The union tells me who I can hire and how and when. And on top of all that, I just got married."

* * *

Employer: "We need a responsible man for the job."

Job Applicant: "That's me. Wherever I've worked, if anything went wrong, they told me I was responsible."

* * *

Detective: "Can you give a description of your missing cashier?"

Banker: "Yes, he's about 5 feet tall and $7,000 short."

* * *

Three men named Johnson, all in the same line of business, opened shops next door to one another. The one on the right had "Johnson" painted in large letters over the door. The one on the left immediately did the same thing. The sign painter then approached the center Mr. Johnson, asking him if he would like his name painted also.

"No," he answered. "I want you to paint the word 'Entrance' over my door."

* * *

I went to the bank and said to the teller that I'd like to check my balance. So she pushed me.

* * *

A man walked into a shoe store and tried on a pair of shoes. "How do they feel?" asked the sales clerk.

"Well . . . they feel a bit tight," replied the man.

The clerk bent down and looked at the shoes and the man's feet. "Try pulling the tongue out," offered the clerk.

"Theyth sthill feelth a bith tighth," he replied.

* * *

Employee: "Boss, can I have the day off tomorrow?"

Boss: "So you want a day off. Let's take a look at what you are asking for:

There are 365 days per year available for work. There are 52 weeks per year in which you already have 2 days off per week, leaving 261 days available for work.

Since you spend 16 hours each day away from work, you have used up 170 days, leaving only 91 days available.

You spend 30 minutes each day on coffee break which counts for 23 days each year, leaving only 68 days available.

With a 1 hour lunch each day, you use up another 46 days, leaving only 22 days available for work.

You normally spend 2 days per year on sick leave.

This leaves you only 20 days per year available for work.

We are off 5 holidays per year, so your available working time is down to 15 days.

We generously give 14 days vacation per year which leaves only 1 day available for work and I'll be darned if you are going to take that day off!"

*   *   *

Signs in Businesses:

In a restaurant: Customers who consider our waitresses uncivil ought to see the manager.

At a loan company: Ask about our plans for owning your home.

In a funeral parlor: Ask about our layaway plan.

In a cemetery: Persons are prohibited from picking flowers from any but their own graves.

Ask Me a Question

How do crazy people go through the forest?
They take the psycho path.

How do you make antifreeze?
Steal her blanket.

What did the hotdog say when he crossed the finish line?
"I'm a wiener! I'm a wiener!"

What's the difference between boogers and broccoli?
You can't get kids to eat broccoli.

What goes "ha ha thump"?
Someone laughing their head off.

What lies at the bottom of the ocean and twitches?
A nervous wreck.

What should you do if you're attacked by a gang of clowns?
Go for the juggler.

What did baby corn say to mama corn?
"Where's pop corn?"

Why did Cinderella get kicked off the soccer team?
Because she ran away from the ball.

What did the paper clip say to the magnet?
"I find you very attractive."

How long have you been working for the company?

Ever since they threatened to fire me.

How can you tell you're getting old?

You go to an antiques auction and three people bid on you.

Did you hear about the two silk worms who were in a race?

They ended up in a tie.

What did one hat say to another?

"You stay there, I'll go on a head."

What do you call a wandering caveman?

A meanderthal.

What do Mack the Knife, Winnie the Pooh, and Attila the Hun have in common?

Same middle name.

What nation's capital is growing the fastest?

Ireland's. It's Dublin every year.

What is brown and sticky?

A stick.

What do you get when you put a candle in a suit of armor?

A knight light.

What do you get when you cross an elephant with a crow?

Downed power lines.

What do they call pastors in Germany?

German Shepherds.

What do you have if there are 100 rabbits standing in a row and 99 take a step back?

A receding hare line.

Why do so many people visit Switzerland?

I don't know, but the flag is a big plus.

Do female frogs croak?

If you hold their little heads under water long enough.

What do you call a boomerang that doesn't come back?

A stick.

While visiting China, your tour guide starts shouting "Poo! Poo! Poo!" What does this mean?

Cattle crossing.

What has 18 legs and catches flies?

A baseball team.

Where does a baseball player go when he needs a new uniform?

New Jersey.

Why did the chicken cross the road halfway?

She wanted to lay it on the line.

Why did the nurse always carry a red pen?

To draw blood.

Did you hear about the geography teacher who wet his bed?

His only weakness was incontinence.

Where do you find a dog with no legs?

Right where you left him.

Why do gorillas have big nostrils?

Because they have big fingers.

What do you get if you cross mistletoe and a duck?

A Christmas Quacker.

What nationality is Santa Claus?

North Polish.

Why are married women heavier than single women?

Because single women come home, see what's in the fridge and go to bed, whereas married women come home, see what's in the bed and go to the fridge!

What do you call cheese that isn't yours?

Nacho Cheese.

What do you call four bull fighters in quicksand?

Quatro sinko.

Why was the writer in agony?

Because her editor removed her colon.

Why did the chicken run onto the soccer field?

Because the referee blew his whistle for a fowl.

What did the elephant say to his girlfriend?

"I love you a ton!"

Why do scuba divers always fall backwards off their boats?

If they fell forward, they'd still be in the boat.

What's the worst thing about living on O street?

Having to go a block to P.

Where does the one-legged woman work?

At I-Hop.

Why was the horse so happy?

Because he lived in a stable environment.

Who won the skeleton beauty contest?

No body.

Support bacteria? Why should I support bacteria?

They're the only culture some people have.

I'm two months pregnant now. When will my baby move?

With any luck, right after he finishes college.

Does pregnancy cause hemorrhoids?

Pregnancy causes anything you want to blame it for.

What did the buffalo say to his little boy when he dropped him off at school?

"Bison."

What did the daddy tomato say to the baby tomato?

"Catch up!"

What was the worst thing about ancient Mesopotamian orators?

They tended to Babylon.

What's the right thing to do when a chemist dies?

Barium.

Why didn't the turkey want any Thanksgiving dinner?

He was already stuffed!

Why did the tire have a nervous breakdown?

It couldn't take any more pressure.

Why was the computer exhausted?

It had a hard drive.

Cannibal one: Am I too late for dinner?

Cannibal two: Yes, everybody's eaten.

Why do roosters crow so early in the morning?

Because they can't get in a word after the hens get up?

What do a tornado and a redneck divorce have in common?

Somebody's gonna lose a trailer!

If a chicken crosses the road, rolls in the dust, and then crosses back, what is she?

A dirty double-crosser.

What's the difference between a Rottweiler and your mother?

Eventually the Rottweiler lets go.

Have you lived here all your life?

Not yet.

Man: I would go to the end of the world for you.

Woman: Yes, but would you stay there?

What do you call two men on the wall above the window?

Kurt and Rod.

What did the Buddhist say to the hot dog vendor?

Make me one with everything.

What did the judge say when a skunk wandered into court?

He banged his gavel and said, "Odor in the courtroom!"

What do you call a lawyer with an IQ of 50?

Your Honor.

Teacher: Billy, name one important thing we have today that we didn't have ten years ago.

Billy: Me!

What is the only sport in which the ball is always in the possession of the team on defense, and the offensive team can score without touching the ball?

Baseball.

Doctor, doctor, I'm a tepee, I'm a wigwam, I'm a tepee, I'm a wigwam.

Relax . . . you're two tents.

What kind of man was Boaz before he married?

Ruthless.

Who was the greatest financier in the Bible?

Noah. He was floating his stock while everyone else was in liquidation.

Why didn't they play cards on the Ark?

Because Noah was standing on the deck.

What kind of motor vehicles are in the Bible?

God drove Adam and Eve out of the Garden in a Fury. David's Triumph was heard throughout the land. And the apostles were all in one Accord.

Who was the greatest comedian in the Bible?

Samson. He brought the house down.

Who is the greatest baby sitter mentioned in the Bible?

David. He rocked Goliath to sleep.

Which servant of God was the most flagrant lawbreaker in the Bible?

Moses. He broke all 10 commandments at once.

What excuse did Adam give to his children as to why he no longer lived in Eden?

Your mother ate us out of house and home.

THE END

Please consider writing a review of this book and posting it at the website on which you purchased it or at your favorite online bookstore.